WITHDRAWN

THE
LABOR
MOVEMENT

UNIONIZING AMERICA

REFORM MOVEMENTS
IN AMERICAN
HISTORY

THE
LABOR
MOVEMENT

UNIONIZING AMERICA

Tim McNeese

CHELSEA HOUSE
PUBLISHERS
An imprint of Infobase Publishing

Cover: Construction workers strike in support of higher wages, circa 1930.

The Labor Movement: Unionizing America

Copyright © 2008 by Infobase Publishing

All rights reserved. No part of this book may be reproduced or utilized in any form or by any means, electronic or mechanical, including photocopying, recording, or by any information storage or retrieval systems, without permission in writing from the publisher. For information contact:

Chelsea House
An imprint of Infobase Publishing
132 West 31st Street
New York NY 10001

Library of Congress Cataloging-in-Publication Data
McNeese, Tim.
  The labor movement : unionizing America / Tim McNeese.
    p. cm. — (Reform movements in American history)
  Includes bibliographical references and index.
  ISBN-13: 978-0-7910-9503-4 (hardcover)
  ISBN-10: 0-7910-9503-7 (hardcover)
  1. Labor unions—United States—History. 2. Working class—United States—History.
3. Industrial relations—United States—History 4. Labor movement—United States—
History. I. Title.
  HD6508.M383 2007
  331.880973—dc22
                              2007014917

Chelsea House books are available at special discounts when purchased in bulk quantities for businesses, associations, institutions, or sales promotions. Please call our Special Sales Department in New York at (212) 967-8800 or (800) 322-8755.

You can find Chelsea House on the World Wide Web at http://www.chelseahouse.com

Series design by Kerry Casey
Cover design by Ben Peterson

Printed in the United States of America

Bang EJB 10 9 8 7 6 5 4 3 2 1

This book is printed on acid-free paper.

All links and Web addresses were checked and verified to be correct at the time of publication. Because of the dynamic nature of the Web, some addresses and links may have changed since publication and may no longer be valid.

CONTENTS

1

A Time of Change

The year was 1884. Americans had just elected New Yorker Grover Cleveland president, the first Democrat chief executive in nearly 30 years. The Civil War was a 20-year-old memory. The country was booming—people were moving west by the millions, even as an equal number of European immigrants were arriving in the eastern United States to replace them. The country was experiencing great change, growth, advancement, modernization, progress, and a new economic era. For the McCormick family of Chicago, however, an earlier, easier time had long since vanished.

The great patriarch of the family, Cyrus McCormick, who had built a vast industrial empire on a single invention, a reaping machine capable of harvesting field grains mechanically, had just died. He had built his first machine in the 1830s and opened his first factory in Chicago to produce his harvesters by the 1840s. The McCormick Harvesting Machine Company had begun small, with only 23 workers. McCormick himself had worked alongside his employees, and he had known every one of them by name. He and his workers built the company into a success, leading to expansion within the McCormick plant. Within just a few years, the harvester works empolyed 200 workers. Even then, McCormick continued to share a relationship with all those who worked there long enough for him to become acquainted with them.

MC CORMICK.

REAPING MACHINE.

With each passing year, however, the gap between McCormick and his ever-increasing workforce widened. By the onset of the Civil War, the factory was experiencing labor problems. McCormick watched as his employees went on strike for higher wages four times during the war years 1863 and 1864. Each time, the company gave in, losing a battle to its workers. The old days of familiarity between owner and worker, management and labor had come to an end. Eventually, in 1880, Cyrus McCormick retired from the company, leaving his 21-year-old son Cyrus Jr., to run the business. Young Cyrus was, after all, a graduate of Princeton University, with a head for mathematics and economics. The company was now in the hands of the second generation.

CHANGES FOR THE COMPANY

With Cyrus Jr., at the helm, the McCormick Harvesting Machine Company continued to successfully make reapers. During the year of the elder McCormick's death—1884— his reaper was 50 years old and still selling strong. His manufacturing operations that year saw a profit of greater than 70 percent! The production plant cranking out McCormick reapers was a giant operation for its day. The factory and connected facilities stretched across dozens of acres; just the floor space for the plant covered 12 acres. A pair of huge, powerful steam engines provided power for the factory, where, depending on the time of year, as many as 1,300 men might be employed. These industrial workers typically put in 60-hour weeks, working 10 hours

Known as the "father of modern agriculture," Cyrus McCormick invented the first mechanical reaping machine in 1831. By the 1840s, his reaper had become so popular that he moved his base of operations to Chicago, where his company grew exponentially.

a day, except Sunday. Their efforts produced about 1,000 McCormick reapers a week—50,000 annually—and these machines were then put to work in America's fields, helping to bring in the nation's abundant harvests.

A profile of the men who worked in McCormick's plant reveals a multinational picture of relative contentment. The vast majority of his workers were of foreign extraction. About 90 percent were German, Norwegian, or Swedish. They were generally happy to be working for McCormick and contented in their work. They lived in company houses that formed company-owned neighborhoods adjacent to the factory grounds, on streets bearing German and Swedish names. Nearly to a man, these skilled employees were adequately compensated for their labors, thought well of their employer, and were not interested in making significant demands of those who held the reins of economic power over them. The single exception of discontent among this vast number of McCormick workers was a small group who worked in the plant's cavernous foundry—the Molders Local Number 233.

McCORMICK'S FIGHTING IRISH

The molders were nearly all "fighting Irish," according to plant officials.[1] The factory only employed around 90 molders, who cast metal parts for larger machines, such as the harvesters, but their skilled labor made them some of the most important workers in the plant. (The molders were aided by a group of semiskilled laborers of about the same number.) Together, they were a tough lot, and they had been organized in a union for years. They watched McCormick's profit margin like hawks. If the prices of the harvesting machines they helped produce went up, the molders were ready to demand better wages and would threaten a strike to make their wants clear. More than once, the Irish molders had been a thorn in the side of McCormick and his factory managers. Moreover, with the passing of Cyrus McCormick Jr., it was his son Cyrus who would inherit his father's troubles with the men of the Molders Local Number 233.

In December 1884, young Cyrus tried to cut the molders' pay by 15 percent and to institute a 10 percent factory-wide cut for everyone else. At first, the younger McCormick thought he had succeeded in getting the molders to agree to the salary cut. The Irish worked only a few months, though, before taking action. When the factory was at full production for the spring farming season, in March 1885, they asked McCormick to restore their wages to their previous levels. He refused, and they called a strike.

McCormick fired back immediately. He hired strikebreaking molders in the Chicago area to replace the Irish strikers. The replacement workers, called "scabs" by union members who despised such nonunion workers who took their colleagues' jobs, were housed inside the harvester factory grounds, so they would not have to come in and out of the plant and face insults and possible injury from the angry, striking workers.

As the strike stretched on for weeks, the work protest took a significant turn. On April 14, the strikers fought with other McCormick workers inside and outside the harvester plant. That day, agents working for the Pinkerton Detective Agency who had been hired by the factory owner as a private police force were assaulted as they rode a horse-drawn omnibus onto the plant grounds. During the melee, the strikers captured a box of Winchester rifles from the detectives, then passed them on to their fellow laborers. Young Cyrus McCormick suddenly faced a tenuous situation. He appealed to mayor Carter Harrison of Chicago to provide city police to protect his factory and his "scab" workers. The mayor, however, who considered the McCormicks political enemies, refused to help, telling Cyrus Jr. to negotiate with the striking molders. With few options, McCormick finally gave in to the strikers, surrendering to their demand to restore their original wages.

ASSESSING THE BLAME

Even as the Irish strikers won better wages, McCormick emerged from the strike convinced more than ever that the Irish molders were nothing but labor troublemakers, a conclusion with which the Pinkertons agreed. As one Pinkerton agent wrote in an after-strike report: "The assault on the Pinkerton police during the strike of last week was urged by Irishmen, who are employed at McCormick's as molders and helpers. These Irishmen are nearly all members of the Ancient Order of Hibernians, who have a most bitter enmity against the Agency."[2] The agent's report continued: "The Germans who participated in McCormick's strike were merely tools, and the Irish were the real instigators both in inaugurating the strike and in the outrages which followed—and in forcing Mr. McCormick to come to terms at a 15 percent increase."[3]

The Pinkerton report was all McCormick needed to form his opinion of the strike and what he would do next to ensure that the Irish molders would not be a problem for him in the future. He would fight not only to meet the antagonistic strategies of the "fighting Irish" he employed, but he would also work to destroy the molders union.

That summer, McCormick took his most important step regarding the skilled Irish workers. He purchased a dozen new pneumatic molding machines capable of performing many of the tasks the molders performed with their hands. That August, just four months after the conclusion of that spring's strike, McCormick closed his plant while the machines were installed. (August and September were usually light months for labor at the factory, so no one had any idea that McCormick was up to something.) When the factory reopened, young Cyrus was able to release the majority of the Irish union members, so that "not one molder who had participated in the spring strike was back on the payroll."[4]

Cyrus McCormick Jr. was certain he had scored a coup against his bothersome Irish molders. He was soon grappling with another problem, however. The machines

With the death of Cyrus McCormick in 1884, control of the McCormick Harvesting Machine Company fell to his son Cyrus Jr. Unlike his father, McCormick Jr. had to deal with a new breed of workers—those who were union members.

meant to save him trouble did not work properly. They broke constantly, causing delays in production and necessitating endless work to repair them. Prior to the installation of the machines, weekly expenses payroll at the harvester plant was $3,000. During the first six months the pneumatic molding machines were on the job, weekly expenses mushroomed to $8,000. Although the molding machines were a general failure economically (McCormick had to hire new molders to oversee the machines), the Irish workers were still gone.

REORGANIZING FOR A FIGHT

In the meantime, the displaced Irish molders were not taking McCormick's action lightly. One of their leaders, a longtime union organizer named Myles McPadden, had been quietly working on a response strategy for the molders. He had been recruiting workers from the McCormick factory to join a union. By February 1886, nearly every skilled craft worker in the plant had joined the Metalworkers Union. In addition, many of the unskilled laborers had joined a large, influential, national union called the Knights of Labor. That month, 1,100 of the 1,400 workers at the McCormick plant became unionized. Many were discontented because they saw what happened to the molders. They had chosen not to cower in fear, however. They had chosen to fight back. New battle lines were being drawn.

By mid-February, the three main unions representing the workers at the McCormick factory—the old Molders Union, the Metalworkers organization, and the Knights of Labor— called a meeting with McCormick to present him with a list of demands. They were simple and straightforward:

> First, that all wages of laboring men be advanced from $1.25 to $1.50 a day. Second, that all vise hands [those

who used a metal-holding tool called a vise] be advanced to $2.00 a day, and that blacksmith helpers be advanced to $1.75. Third, that time the men spend in the water closet [the toilet] not be limited as heretofore. Fourth, that, inasmuch as the molding machines are a failure, the preference should be given the old hands. The scabs in the foundry must be discharged, and a pledge given that no man would be discharged for taking part in a strike.[5]

Perhaps surprisingly, McCormick and factory officials were ready to agree to most of the worker demands. But on the fourth demand, they intended to stand fast. They were not prepared to rehire the ousted Irish molders, let the replacement scabs go, or sanction future strikes. The union leaders refused to accept McCormick's terms. They called a strike against McCormick's plant.

The strike received wide support and was well organized. Plant officials, however, seemed equally organized. Factory managers closed down the factory to put pressure on workers to forego their strike. Even as union members prepared to set up their picket lines close to the factory, 400 city police officers were called in to keep the workers at a distance from the plant. (McCormick had recently become a supporter of Mayor Harrison. This time, Harrison provided police support to McCormick against the strikers.) The company even provided meals to the policemen, and McCormick could sometimes be seen filling the coffee cups of the law enforcement officers. When the factory reopened after being shut down for two weeks, McCormick only allowed nonunion workers to come back to work. Only a few hundred reported for work, however; McCormick was losing money every day.

Weeks turned into months, and the strike continued. The union members walking the picket lines and supporting the strike knew what was at stake and that they must not fail. The future of unions at the McCormick plant hung in the balance. Every new day of the strike, though, meant that workers were struggling even more than before to survive and to feed their families. The workers could take comfort that they were not alone in their efforts. That spring, strikes were spreading throughout Chicago, as other factories and businesses struggled with their own labor issues. Then, the various unions in and around the city called for a general strike on behalf of the eight-hour workday. The day for the citywide event was set for May 1. It was at this juncture that the strike at the McCormick plant became part of a larger, generalized labor protest involving not only workers at the harvester facility, but also thousands of skilled and unskilled disgruntled laborers throughout northern Illinois.

A RADICAL ELEMENT

The strike was gigantic in scope. Workers were uniting everywhere, hoping to bring about significant change for themselves and their working conditions, but the general strike also brought out a more radical element of workers. On May 3, a mass rally was organized by a group of lumber workers; it was to be held on Black Road, not far from the McCormick factory. The rally would include a speech by a hard-nosed, radical labor agitator—August Spies.

Spies was not a new immigrant; he had left his home in Landeck, Germany, in 1872, while still quite young. Once he had arrived in New York as "a well-tutored youth of seventeen,"[6] Spies took his first American job in a German-owned upholstery shop. Soon, however, he was wandering around his new country, taking other work, until he landed in Chicago, where he found a thriving German community. Once again, he returned to furniture upholstery, because the city's "150 furniture factories employed more than 4,000 workers, while several hundred more skilled hands toiled in 19 upholstery shops."[7] Spies found a place for himself among his fellow Germans on Chicago's North Side, where the immigrant population operated saloons, grocery stores, butcher shops, bakeries, tobacco stores, and churches, as well as larger businesses, such as furniture and upholstery shops. Spies stood out among his peers as a young man, now 20, who loved gymnastics and kept himself in great physical condition, "even though he drank several schooners of lager beer each day."[8] He doted on his great, curving, pompadour hair, fussed with his long mustaches, loved dancing on Saturday nights, and was comfortable with the ladies. Spies was soon recognized "as a young man who would make good in Chicago."[9] During the following decade, Spies became recognized as a leader among a growing group of German socialists in the Chicago area.

Before the end of his first year in Chicago, Spies was drawn into the socialist movement and began reading everything he could get his hands on concerning socialism. By the late 1870s, Spies purchased his own upholstery shop. As a business owner, he had plenty of time to make the rounds in the German beer gardens and saloons to talk to working-men, laborers, and tradesmen, preaching the gospel of social organization and the power of the working class to take control of their own destinies. Even as early as 1877, Spies had participated in violent labor disputes and joined a radical, armed organization of workers. By the mid-1880s, he was considered an extremist.

At the time, Spies was working more as a radical writer than a radical workingman. He was the editor of a German-language, socialist newspaper and a member of the Socialist Labor Party. By coming to the rally on Black Road, Spies hoped to encourage the workers on strike by delivering a strong speech. During his speech, violence broke out between striking workers and their nonunion, "scab" replacements, who were spotted leaving the plant at the end of their afternoon shifts. Many of the scabs fled back into the McCormick plant for their own protection, only to be followed by the angry strikers, who began smashing windows. During the violent confrontation, 200 police officers appeared on the scene and began firing into the demonstrating strikers. In the aftermath of the bloody encounter, four workers lay dead and others were wounded.

Emotions were running high among the workers, and Spies leapt into action. The following day, the very newspaper he worked for began printing circulars, calling for a massive rally of workers, to be held at Chicago's Haymarket. The first batch of circulars read as follows:

Attention Workingmen!

GREAT

MASS-MEETING

TO-NIGHT, at 7.30 o'clock,

------------ AT THE ------------

HAYMARKET, Randolph St., Bet. Desplaines and Halsted.

Good Speakers will be present to denounce the latest atrocious act of the police, the shooting of our fellow-workingmen yesterday afternoon.

Workingmen Arm Yourselves and Appear in Full Force!

THE EXECUTIVE COMMITTEE

In all, of the 20,000 circulars printed, only about 200 included the call for workers to show up at the rally armed. Spies himself would not agree to come to the Haymarket and address the expected crowd until that line had been removed from the circular.

VIOLENCE IN HAYMARKET SQUARE

That evening, Spies arrived at Haymarket Square around 8:30 and was immediately disappointed. The Haymarket had been chosen as the site for the rally because it was large enough for 20,000 people to gather there, but only a few thousand were present when Spies reached the square. He did not hesitate to take control of the crowd that had gathered, however. The 31-year-old Spies climbed up on a wagon and began to speak. Soon, the disappointing crowd became intent on his message: "The fight is going on. Now is the chance to strike for the oppressed classes. The oppressors want us to be content. They will kill us. The day is not far distant when we will resort to hanging these men." Applause passed through the crowd, along with cries of "Hang them now." Spies continued: "McCormick is the man who created the row on Monday, and he must be held responsible for the murder of our brothers!"[10]

For almost an hour, Spies continued his speech, using the moment and the momentum of the past few days to inspire anger and solidarity in those who heard his words in the Haymarket. Then, a second speaker took center stage, Albert R. Parsons, a socialist associate of Spies. He, too, was a radical journalist, and his words were as strong as his comrade's, and even more dramatic: "I am not here for the purpose of inciting anybody, but to speak out, to tell the facts . . . even though it shall cost me my life before morning. It

On May 4, 1886, August Spies organized a rally in Chicago's Haymarket Square in response to the deaths of four workers who had been shot by police after they walked off the job at McCormick Harvesting Machine Company on May 3. During the rally, an unidentified person threw a bomb into the crowd, which killed one police officer and injured a number of others. Pictured are the five men who were accused of being behind the bomb plot. Clockwise from top left: August Spies, Louis Lingg, Albert Parsons, Adolph Fischer, and George Engel.

behooves you . . . Americans, in the interest of your liberty and independence, to *arm*, to *arm* yourselves!"[11]

Even as Spies and Parsons spoke to the crowd of working-class men who had gathered, they were unaware that there were several hundred Chicago police officers listening to their fiery words. Parsons's call to his audience to arm themselves was ironic. The law enforcement officers were already carrying weapons. The mayor of Chicago was also present, unrecognized by the crowd. Once Mayor Harrison decided that the rally would remain peaceful, he left the square. Only then did the police officers make their move, calling for the gathered crowd to disperse. The order was almost too late, for many in the crowd were already leaving, even as a third speaker was readying to take his turn. The time was nearly 10:30 P.M.

Suddenly, someone tossed something into the crowd toward the police. In seconds, the fiery fuse burned down, and the homemade dynamite bomb exploded with a loud blast, sending the crowd into a panic. Several police officers lay on the brick street, one dead and others hurt. Stunned, the remaining law enforcement officers reorganized and began firing into the crowd. Others swung clubs at the shouting, frightened onlookers. The violence lasted only a few minutes, but, when the smoke lifted, Haymarket Square was empty, except for nearly 80 victims, including a handful of dead and a larger number of wounded.

What had happened in the Haymarket that fateful evening? Who was responsible? Why had a simple strike in support of an eight-hour workday for workers in Chicago led to two armed clashes between regular, working-class Americans and law enforcement officers? At the time, the labor movement was still struggling to establish itself and become accepted. As the toll from the violence in the Haymarket was assessed, with all sides—workers, factory owners, city officials, Chicago police officers, and radicals—alike pointing fingers at one another, holding one another to blame, the country's workers could only imagine how many more decades it would take before they would gain their rights. During the coming years, America's laborers would fight for better working conditions, higher pay, fewer hours, and a modicum of respect. However in the aftermath of the Haymarket, the struggle for workers' rights seemed to be a daunting proposition.

2

Labor in Early America

During the 1600s, Europeans immigrated to North America by the tens of thousands, and the vast majority of them came to the New World with at least one common understanding—once they reached the colony of their choice, they would have to work hard. Life in colonial America was often difficult, requiring long days of backbreaking labor. Colonists hammered out metal goods as blacksmiths; loaded and unloaded cargo off the great wooden merchant ships that regularly reached harbors from Boston to Savannah; cleared land for farming by cutting down the heavy virgin timber; put in long hours as craftsmen and -women, producing everything from barrels to wagons, furniture to yarn; and sweated under the heat of coal-fired iron forges. The colonies needed the skilled labor of carpenters and bricklayers, distillers and malters, sailmakers and shipwrights, tanners and weavers, shoemakers and tailors, smiths and coopers, and glaziers and printers. Work was the colonial constant.

Although skilled workers were always in great demand, there was a greater need for unskilled labor, often provided by those who worked as indentured servants. It was customary, especially during the 1600s and early 1700s, for European immigrants to reach America with little money in their pockets and few skills at their disposal. They could not afford land once they arrived in the New World, even though the vast majority of them had worked as farmers in the Old Country. A system was created to provide such poor, unskilled would-be immigrants the opportunity to find work in America. If they were unable to afford the cost of their ship passage, a sponsor, often someone already established in America, could pay the passage. In exchange, the new immigrant would sign a contract allowing himself or herself to be "indentured" to their sponsor for a period of time.

Indentures typically lasted for seven years, and the labor the indentured servant provided would help pay off his or her debt. Indentured servants were often not only poor, but young, unmarried, and had little professional work experience. They were not paid wages but were provided room and board during their indenture. Once the indenture was completed, such a servant was considered to have paid his or her debt and was free to leave his master and seek his or her fortune. Thousands of Europeans served as indentured servants; they provided temporary but vital labor for the colonies and their economic development and progress.

Another labor force was also in practice in the colonies, and its nature was, perhaps, the most unique of any in the Americas. These workers were black slaves, forcefully taken from their African homes by slave catchers, who then sold them to European traders along the coast of West Africa. Unlike other workers, black slaves did not choose to work under such limited and abusive conditions—they were forced to do so. The labor provided by black slaves would exist in all the 13 British colonies, especially in the southern colonies, and the numbers were significant.

Between 1500 and 1850, Europeans imported about 10 million slaves to the New World. (An additional 2 million were also removed from Africa, but died on the "Middle Passage" voyage across the Atlantic, before arriving in the

Americas.) Of that number, about 5 percent (500,000) were delivered to the 13 English colonies. Slavery did not take root in the British colonies for many decades. Most black slaves reached North America after 1700. In that year, the number of slaves in the 13 colonies stood at 25,000. By the opening year of the American Revolution (1775), however, slaves numbered about a half million. (Many were not imported to the colonies but were born here as the children of slave parents, the result of natural increase.) Of those 500,000 slaves, 90 percent labored in the southern colonies of Virginia, Maryland, Georgia, and the two Carolinas.

THE DOMINANCE OF FREE LABOR

Black slaves and indentured servants were significant labor forces in the British colonies of North America. These two groups did not make up the portion of the colonial labor force that could be referred to as "free labor," those who worked at jobs of their choosing, sometimes receiving wages for their efforts. With each passing decade of the colonial period (1607–1776), the numbers of free men and women in the workforce continued to rise steadily. Such workers might be immigrants who reached America as free individuals with enough money to buy land to farm or establish themselves in a business or craft; those who had completed their indentures; Indians who sought work among European colonists after being forced off their lands; free blacks, some of whom had earlier been slaves; and the children and descendants of all those groups.

The largest group of free laborers in early America was those who "made a living through a family farm, a family craft shop, or some combination of the two."[12] Even in the earliest years of the colonies, though, some laborers worked as wage earners. By the 1700s, the percentage of colonists

THE
Country Housewife
AND
LADY's DIRECTOR,
IN THE
Management of a House, and the
Delights and Profits of a Farm.

CONTAINING

INSTRUCTIONS for managing the Brew-
House, and Malt-Liquors in the Cellar; the
making of Wines of all sorts.

DIRECTIONS for the DAIRY, in the Improvement
of Butter and Cheese upon the worst of Soils;
the feeding and making of Brawn; the ordering
of Fish, Fowl, Herbs, Roots, and all other useful Branches belonging to a Country-Seat, in the
most elegant manner for the Table.

Practical OBSERVATIONS concerning DISTILLING;
with the best Method of making Ketchup, and many
other curious and durable Sauces.

The whole distributed in their proper MONTHS, from the
Beginning to the End of the Year.

With particular REMARKS relating to the Drying or Kilning of
SAFFRON.

By R. BRADLEY,
Professor of Botany in the University of Cambridge,
and F. R. S.

The Sixth Edition.
With ADDITIONS.

LONDON:
Printed for D. BROWNE, at the Black-Swan without Temple-Bar.
MDCCXXXVI.
[Price 2s. 6d.]

During America's colonial era, most laborers made their living by farming or working in a family craft shop. Many of these new English immigrants used the *Country Housewife and Lady's Director in the Management of a House, and the Delights and Profits of a Farm* to help them learn how to subsist in their new homeland.

who were paid wages was steadily growing, especially in the coastal cities and smaller towns. Chief among those working for wages were sailors, artisans, and craftspeople; women and girls who worked in the limited cloth and clothing production industry; men and boys who were employed as field hands, freight haulers, and construction workers; and others who were collectively referred to as "common labor."

AMERICAN WAGE EARNERS

Receiving wages for work often did not mean that the workers had good-paying jobs. Most common laborers were poorly paid, the exception being journeyworkers who were highly skilled. (By definition, a journeyperson was a skilled worker who had learned his or her craft as an apprentice, which made one qualified to practice the trade.) The labor of the common workers was often devalued, even though "nearly all earned substantially more than their European counterparts."[13]

Household servants and hired farmworkers often lived with their employers and were provided food and shelter, but they were expected to work 16-hour days and were paid little money. Even when they took jobs in the urban colonial centers, such as Boston, New York, Philadelphia, or Charleston, the wages for common laborers were low. In Philadelphia, for example, although it was one of the most prosperous cities in the colonies, common laborers often earned no more than 50 pounds annually, less than a pound a week. This was 10 pounds less than the amount that a family in Philadelphia needed to survive. This meant that wives and children of male common laborers had to find jobs themselves to make the family's ends meet. Single women with children were often at the bottom of the workforce and were required to work jobs that barely provided enough money for food and shelter for their families.

Although new immigrants arrived in colonial America constantly, there were few labor organizations that protected workers. Those that did exist were often little more than groups formed by people who practiced the same skilled trade or craft. Several such organizations were established by master craftspeople and skilled carpenters, among the highest wage earners in the colonies. The largest such organization was chartered in 1724—the Carpenters' Company of Philadelphia. This labor group functioned much like a guild, setting the prices that carpenters could charge for their work, the rate they could pay those who worked for them, and the rules directing their treatment of young apprentices learning their craft. Such labor organizations provided other benefits, as well. Some of "these societies provided members with sick benefits, small loans, and assistance in times of dire need."[14]

Some skilled workers formed their own labor organizations. In 1741, the Journeyman Caulkers of Boston was established to provide a united front through which they could make demands on the master craftsmen who employed them. (The Boston group was specifically formed to force their masters to stop paying them with promissory notes— paper notes promising payment later—rather than paying them up front.) Sometimes, journeymen and craftsmen alike formed such labor organizations to protest colonial laws that placed "artificial" ceilings on the prices such skilled workers could charge for their services. Carters, coopers (barrel makers), bakers, and chimney sweeps were among those restricted by such statutes, and they sometimes took action together against such restrictions. Sometimes, their protests were violent.

The actions of workers did not typically escalate to walking off the job which would become a much more widely used labor tactic during the late nineteenth century. Work stoppages were used by skilled workers, however, to put pressure on colonial leaders to remove labor-price controls. Among the most notorious for their work stoppages and perhaps the most militant of all colonial wage earners were sailors. These independent-minded laborers often "displayed a legendary contempt for wielders of arbitrary authority, from constables to kings."[15] (Perhaps it was this trait that drew thousands of sailors to become pirates, who plundered the ships of wealthy merchants or European powers.) Sailors were known for their solidarity, because they worked so closely together onboard ships and were dependent on one another more so than those in any other labor setting. It was not uncommon for disgruntled, demanding sailors to abandon a ship with nearly every mate cooperating in the work stoppage. Such actions might leave a ship owner or shipping merchant with ships stranded in port unable to sail out or even be maintained while docked. Sailors might strike, even while at sea, in protest of unsafe work conditions, harsh punishments such as floggings, capricious captains, or for longer periods of time in port once their ship docked. Work stoppages among sailors were so common, in fact, that their actions fostered the word *strike*. When sailors made the decision to stop working, they would "strike," or lower the ship's sails, leaving a ship at sea dead in the water until an agreement could be made with a ship's captain or owner.

NEW OPPORTUNITIES FOR COLONIAL LABOR

During the second half of the eighteenth century, workers in the British colonies of North America would experience new opportunities for themselves, brought on, in part, by the American Revolution. Work, for an increasing number of Americans, was becoming about working in manufacturing, even if their workplaces were little more than small mills and factories. Although the southern economy remained dependent on tobacco-based agriculture and slave labor, more workers in the New England colonies (Massachusetts, Connecticut, Rhode Island, and New Hampshire) and the Middle colonies (New York, New Jersey, and Pennsylvania) were taking jobs as both unskilled and skilled wage earners in textile plants, shipyards, ropewalks, paper mills, gunpowder factories, grain mills, and distilleries than in earlier years.

It was the beginning of larger-scale manufacturing in America. After 1750, ironworks established in

(continues on page 32)

COLONIAL LABOR PROTESTS

Although true labor unions in America did not really take root until the early nineteenth century, the workers of the colonial period were sometimes so dissatisfied with their working conditions or their wages that they banded together in protest. These colonial calls for improvements for themselves as workers formed the early history of American labor protests.

Perhaps the earliest labor protest on record in the American colonies took place within a generation of British colonizing along the Atlantic Coast. In 1636, a group of Maine fishermen chose to protest their work conditions to their employer, Robert Trelawney. The fishermen, working off the coast of Maine on Richmond Island, chose to fall "into a mutany"* when Trelawney withheld their wages from them. Although the group was small and their protest barely remembered, it did represent cooperative action resulting in a work stoppage.

Nearly 40 years later, in New York City, another labor protest took place. The licensed cartmen of the city, contracted to haul refuse and dirt from the town's streets, walked off the job because of low wages. To protest their pay, they "combined to refuse full compliance."** Contemporary records of the 1760s and 1770s tell of similar work stoppages and protests by American work groups. In 1768, New York's journeymen tailors engaged in a "turnout," a work protest similar to the modern-day strike. In this case, about two dozen tailors struck against their employers to protest a reduction of their wages. Serious about their strike, the journeymen published ads in local newspapers, offering their services as tailors, in defiance of the master tailors they worked for. Working out of their base in a New York tavern called the Sign of the Fox and Hound, they set their new wages at three shillings and six pence a day, plus a daily food ration.

Sometimes, craft masters themselves engaged in labor protests. One such group of nearly three dozen Bostonian barbers joined together to raise their prices for shaving by 25 percent, from 8 shillings to 10. In addition, they also decided to "advance 5s. On the Price of making common Wiggs and 10s. On their Tye ones."*** The organized

group of barbers also decided that "no one of their Faculty should shave or dress Wiggs on Sunday morning." [†]

During the American Revolution, with wartime inflation bringing new protests by American labor, yet another New York group, this time the city's printers, made demands in 1778 for an increase in their wages. They ran ads in support of their demands in the papers, including the city's *Royal Gazette*. In these ads, the printers explained their circumstances:

> As the necessaries of life are raised to such an enormous price, it cannot be expected that we should continue to work at the wages now given; and therefore request an addition of Three Dollars per week to our present small pittance. . . . There is not one among us, we trust, that would take an ungenerous advantage of the times—we only wish barely to exist, which it is impossible to do with our present stipend. [††]

There would be additional labor protests during the colonial period and the years of the American Revolution. Sailors in Philadelphia struck in 1779 and New York cobblers six years later. Journeymen printers protested their wages in 1786, calling for wages of $6 per week. Such work stoppages, protests, and strikes would only help to create the true labor organizations that would become commonplace in the United States over the following century—these became known as labor unions.

Shoemakers in Philadelphia were among the first to create such an organization, in 1792. Their first attempt to organize did not survive past its first anniversary, only to be resurrected in 1794. This time, the efforts of the shoemakers paid off and their organization carried them into the nineteenth century. Other shoemakers formed similar organizations between 1794 and 1818 in cities that included New York, Philadelphia, Baltimore, and Pittsburgh. New York printers, a labor force that had engaged in earlier work stoppages, banded together in 1794, creating a permanent organization they called a

(continues)

(continued)

"Typographical Society." As with the shoemakers, printers in other cities—including Boston, New York, Albany, Philadelphia, Baltimore, Washington City, and New Orleans—established their own permanent labor organizations. Other trades followed suit, including Philadelphia cabinetmakers and carpenters and Baltimore tailors.

With nearly every one of these early labor organizations, the structure was almost entirely local and the members of the organization limited to those who worked in that one craft.

---

* Foster Rhea Dulles and Melvyn Dubofsky, *Labor in America, A History* (Arlington Heights, Ill.: Harlan Davidson, 1984), 21.

** Ibid.

*** Ibid.

† Ibid

†† Ibid., 21–22.

(continued from page 29)

Pennsylvania, Maryland, and New Jersey employed many more workers than previously. One such iron production system was established by Peter Hasenclever, who would gain a reputation as one of the greatest colonial ironmasters of the eighteenth century. His operation included six small-scale blast furnaces, seven forges, and a stamping mill. He employed 500 workers, many of whom he recruited directly from iron operations in Germany.

Another new operation was a glass works built in Manheim, Pennsylvania, by Henry Stiegel. Although the size of his workforce is not known, his glass factory was large enough "that a coach and four could turn around within the brick dome of its melting house."[16]

Factories to produce linen cloth were built, some housing as many as 14 looms. Another textile "manufacturing house" operating in Boston by the late 1760s housed 400 spinning wheels. Another, larger, textile plant was in business by 1775, the year the American Revolution began. Operated by the United Company of Philadelphia for Promoting American Manufacture, this textile mill employed 400 female spinners producing cotton goods.

During the American Revolution (1775–1783), laborers in America received a boost. The war attracted tens of thousands of men into the ranks of the Continental Army to fight against the British. With the resulting labor shortage, wage earners and others saw their wages go up accordingly. The change was so significant that patriot leaders tried to establish price and wage controls in several colonies, especially the New England colonies. In 1776, it was decided that farmworkers should not be paid more than three

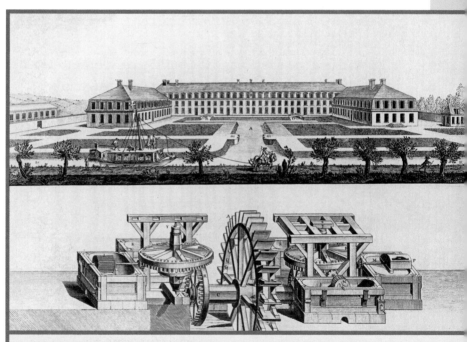

After the first paper mill was established in America in 1690, the industry quickly became one of the primary sources of employment for both skilled and unskilled workers in the Middle and New England colonies. This eighteenth-century engraving depicts a colonial paper mill.

shillings and four pence for a day's labor, an amount three times higher than such workers could anticipate receiving a century earlier. The wages for artisans, mechanics, and various skilled labor was set at an equivalent rate of change as that of the rates received by farm laborers. Such wages were never very high during the 1770s and 1780s, though, when the war with Great Britain was raging and the future of the American colonies remained uncertain. Even after the war was over and an American victory assured, wage earners continued to work for limited incomes. Even though one of the Founding Fathers, John Jay, who would become the first chief justice of the new U.S. Supreme Court, wrote in 1784 that "the wages of mechanics and laborers . . . are very extravagant," they were rarely paid more than 15 shillings weekly, a figure equal to less than four dollars.[17]

Even as the American Revolution brought new economic freedoms to workers from New Hampshire to Georgia, with democracy replacing the limits placed on the colonies by British authorities, this new form of government did not guarantee a better standard of living for many in America. Historian John Bach McMaster described the working conditions of many workers after the smoke of the revolution cleared:

> On such a pittance it was only by the strictest economy that a mechanic kept his children from starvation and himself from jail. In the low and dingy rooms which he called his home were wanting many articles of adornment and of use now to be found in the dwellings of the poorest of his class. Sand sprinkled on the floor did duty as a carpet. There was no glass on his table, there was no china in his cupboard, there were no prints on his walls. What a stove was he did not know, coal he had never seen, matches he had never heard of . . . He rarely tasted fresh meat as often as once a week, and paid for it a much higher price than his posterity.[18]

In many ways, labor conditions improved for the average worker following the American Revolution. Post-Revolutionary War America was a land of great opportunity, one in which artisans, mechanics, and skilled and unskilled laborers might be able to improve their lives. Many of them looked forward to better days and improved working and living conditions. Craftspeople were still recognized and respected by many, even if their wages did not reflect it.

Workers often still found it difficult to make ends meet or even to have a say in their working conditions. In addition, the U.S. government of the 1790s, generally under the control of the Federalists, often ruled in the same ways as British authorities and aristocrats had in earlier generations. They passed restrictive laws through Congress that sometimes directly impacted American labor. One such series of laws worked against laborers joining together in common union. In fact, the Federalists built "a legal system based on British law, which treated labor unions as criminal conspiracies."[19] Even as the eighteenth century approached, the true future of American labor appeared uncertain.

America's First Labor Unions

Before workers in the United States could create viable labor organizations, changes had to be made in the basic structure of the American economic system. During the colonial period, the general condition of labor was based on the relationship between master craftspeople and their apprentices and journeypeople, who worked with them on shared projects. Although the master provided both labor groups with wages, this relationship was not that of a true employer and employee. They all were working on the same side of the economic fence. Their stakes in the economy, as well as their interests, were similar, and they labored side by side. By the late 1700s and early 1800s, however, the American economic system experienced significant transformation. The British, removed from the scene by the American Revolution, were no longer governing the colonies and controlling their economies. The new economic system was being redefined "by the rise of merchant capitalists who established business on a wholesale basis."[20]

This fundamental change had an impact on labor, so it helped to encourage and create "permanent" trade or labor unions. Earlier labor issues were addressed with "temporary" remedies, as were those of the New York printers, who went on strike in 1778 to win a wage increase. In the new post-Revolutionary America, especially after the adoption of the U.S. Constitution of 1787 (the earlier constitution, the Articles of Confederation, worked dramatically against free trade), wholesale-order employers began to take over the general economy of the new American republic. The new system developed relatively quickly and was generally accepted:

> The wholesale-order shopkeeper operated in a different economy from his predecessors; his market was highly competitive and he found it impossible to pass increased costs to consumers in the form of increased prices. Instead he found it necessary to reduce his costs. At first he met this problem by asking his journeymen to produce wholesale-order work more cheaply than shopwork. Realizing that their employer had to meet competition, they agreed.[21]

Such concessions on the part of labor would not continue without complaint for long, however. One of the problems was the significant inflation that Americans experienced during George Washington's and John Adams's presidencies. Between 1791 and 1800, the general cost of living in the new United States increased by 30 percent. Suddenly, the demands for wage decreases made by the wholesale-order shopkeeper began to appear unreasonable. With this new economic equation, workers had few choices but to turn increasingly to organizing themselves for their own economic protection. Instead of temporary organizations and stop-gap work stoppages, they began to establish permanent organizations that were typically referred to as "associations" and "societies." Such words would be replaced in later years with the term *labor unions*, which is still used today.

Perhaps the first such "continuous organization," or early trade union of wageworkers, established in the United States occurred in Philadelphia in 1794, with the formation of the Federal Society of Journeymen Cordwainers. (Cordwainers

Between 1791 and 1800, the general rate of inflation skyrocketed in the United States and the cost of living increased by 30 percent. Affluent neighborhoods such as Philadelphia's Society Hill sprung up during this period and served as the center of the upper class. Society Hill's Bingham Mansion, at the corner of Third and Spruce streets, is depicted in this 1800 engraving.

were a specific type of shoemaker who worked with leather.) Its members were exclusively journeymen shoemakers. As an early union, its members engaged in a strike and a picket of masters' shops in 1799.

The craft workers who joined such labor organizations often experienced many of the same circumstances. Once workers became members, they paid their association a fee of perhaps 50¢ or so, then began paying monthly dues of a few pennies. Meetings were held each month (those who did not attend were typically fined), and the members were expected to remain civil and orderly during such meetings. At these meetings, the members of a craft association discussed important issues that, during the early 1800s, might have included setting minimum wages, establishing the number of workers the organization would accept in their craft, and the ongoing problem of competition from workers who were not completely competent in their craft. Such inferior workers were often "runaway apprentices" willing to work for less money.[22]

Once the members of the craft association isolated their most important problems and issues, they then set about trying to settle them. Early union tactics were generally straightforward and simple. Any employers who paid less than the accepted wage scale would be boycotted by the group. In addition, organized workers also tried to create a "closed shop," in which they encouraged employers to hire only members of their association for a specific type of work. Collective bargaining—negotiations that took place in the name of a group or groups of workers, rather than just on behalf of a single laborer—was also practiced. The first early American example involved two labor groups in Philadelphia—shoemakers and cordwainers—who formed a trade agreement together with employers. If workers's demands were not met by negotiation, they might then engage in a strike.

EMPLOYERS FIGHT BACK—IN COURT

As more and more workers associated themselves with these early labor unions, employers did not stand idly by. They turned to the courts to bring down these worker organizations to protect their own interests. Among the most important of these early labor cases was a series of legal battles known as the Cordwainers Conspiracy Cases. Six cases were tried between 1806 and 1815. Only three of

EARLY STRIKES AND VIOLENCE

As workers in the United States became more organized during the 1790s and early 1800s, they often engaged in direct and confrontational tactics to obtain their goals—expectations that might include better work conditions, higher wages, or exclusive agreements from would-be employers that they would only hire association members who practiced a specific skill or craft. Sometimes the tactics these early organized laborers employed would include or lead to violence.

During one work turnout, or strike, by Philadelphia shoemakers, six journeymen decided to remain on the job and keep working. To protect them, their employer hid them in an upstairs room in his shop. The striking shoemakers kept an eye out for the renegade journeymen and finally caught up with them when they came out of their hiding place on a Sunday evening to have a few drinks at a local tavern. Catching them unawares, the strikers beat them up.

On another occasion, a group of organized workers walked off their jobs when their employer offered them wages below the established scale. In response, their employer hired 50 new journeymen to take their places. Not to be outdone, the striking workers established a picket line and forcefully manned it, daring any worker to cross it.

Violence involving rough-and-tumble sailors was a common occurence. During one sailors' strike in New York City, the shipboard workers demanded new wages that would increase their pay from $10 weekly to $14. The striking sailors created such disturbances that local constables were called in to break up the organized laborers. On another occasion, striking New York sailors decided to raid a ship owned by a merchant with whom they were having labor issues. When news of the planned attack spread, a group of local citizens tried to protect the ship in question by manning it against the striking sailors. The result was a violent melee, during which the strikers stormed the ship. They met stiff opposition, and the strikers "were three times repulsed, with broken and bloody noses." *

---

* Joseph G. Rayback, *A History of American Labor* (New York: Free Press, 1966), 29.

the cases were recorded, though, and included those tried in Philadelphia in 1806, in New York three years later, and in Pittsburgh in 1815. The cases came about when journeymen shoemakers, facing low wages and other economic pressures placed on them by their employers, organized together to demand a decent minimum wage. Refusing to budge, the employers went to court to settle the situation, claiming the cordwainers and their various labor organizations constituted nothing more than "conspiracies in restraint of trade under the common law."[23]

Each case had its unique aspects. The Philadelphia case in 1806 featured a dozen cordwainers and a judge who appeared to side with the employers. He spoke in court of the cordwainers' strike as "pregnant with public mischief and private injury."[24] His decision was harsh and did not come as a surprise. In his words: "A combination of workmen to raise their wages may be considered in a two-fold point of view; one is to benefit themselves . . . the other is to injure those who do not join their society. The rule of law condemns both."[25] To the judge, using old common law, the actions of the cordwainers constituted nothing more than a conspiracy, even though they had formed only a labor organization and were seeking only a decent living wage.

The cases that arose in New York and Pittsburgh met the same end. Judges found in favor of the employers and against the shoemakers, charging them with "criminal conspiracy."[26] During the New York case, titled *People v. Melvin*, the court examined the question of whether such a group of workers could band together to seek a raise in wages. The focus was on whether the journeymen's strike was lawful or not. The court determined that the journeymen did have the same rights as everyone in their community, but they did not have the right to utilize methods "of a nature too arbitrary and coercive, and which went to deprive their fellow citizens of rights as precious as any they contended for."[27]

During the Pittsburgh case, the question of what constituted lawful means of coercion was more deeply examined. In that case, the court determined that the cordwainers had created an unlawful conspiracy by having their members "confederate together by direct means to impoverish or prejudice a third person, or to do acts prejudicial to the community."[28] The court also determined the illegality of a labor organization forcing an employer to hire only certain individuals (obviously, those in the labor organization itself), because that potentially prevented the hiring of someone who wanted to ply his trade but chose not to join the labor group.

The upshot of these cases was the destabilization of America's early labor organizations. The court had decided against labor groups that pushed for a closed shop or tried to gain their goals by coercion and intimidation. The cases put so many restrictions on the way such labor groups operated that it was almost impossible for them to be successful. Other circumstances also helped to destroy the infant labor movement. The United States had fought a war with Great Britain, the War of 1812, until 1815, the year of the last of the Cordwainers' cases.

A serious depression followed the war, especially after 1819. In that year alone, it is estimated that 20,000 laborers were unemployed in New York and Philadelphia, and another 10,000 in Baltimore. This created a great problem for labor organizations. Business activity was reduced as prices rose, and the demand for labor likewise declined, even among skilled workers. Such laborers could not expect to strike or hold out for better wages, nor could they expect to force employers to create closed shops. Many became so desperate for jobs that they nearly abandoned all such protests and tactics, regardless of how low the wages were or how poor the working conditions. During these difficult economic years, records indicate that nearly every labor organization collapsed, with one exception: the Columbia Typographical Society, in Washington City, the nation's capital, "where the volume of government printing was hardly affected by hard times."[29]

ORGANIZING FEDERATIONS

American labor did not wait long to reorganize and pick itself back up from its losses in the years following the War of 1812. This new era of labor organization included a couple of new twists. By December 1827, a craft union called the Mechanics' Union of Trade Associations was formed in Philadelphia. It would be the first labor organization in the United States to include workers from more than one trade or craft. Then, by the summer of 1828, the new labor organizers took another bold and innovative step: They formed a grass roots political party called the Working Men's Party and promoted candidates for several state and city offices in Pennsylvania. Calls went out for the members of the union to "take the management of their own interests, as a class, into their own immediate keeping."[30] The Working Men's Party would only prove to be a start. Throughout the 1830s, other labor-based political parties were formed in as many as 60 cities and communities from Cincinnati to Washington, D.C., to Portland, Maine. These parties of laborers supported such issues as the repeal of conspiracy laws that harmed labor unions, more public schools, an end to compulsory service in state militias, and other reforms that were of a vested interest to the country's laboring interests. They also supported, generally, such political goals as the 10-hour workday, voting rights for all adult white men, abolition of imprisonment as a punishment for debt, and destruction of all large businesses that represented little more than "chartered monopolies."[31]

All these new labor parties were organized on the local level, so their individual scope and influence typically remained limited and regional. During Andrew Jackson's presidency (1829–37), the Democratic Party, took on the same causes supported by these smaller labor parties and encourage laborers to vote for the national party. Nevertheless, craftspeople and skilled workers continued to organize their own local parties. But, overall, such political organizations barely survived the 1830s.

The 1830s did prove to be a boon to the new craft unions. Between 1831 and 1836, new trade organizations came into existence for the first time or were revived after a dormant period of economic downturn. At least 200 trade associations were established during this five-year period, with a combined membership estimated at between 100,000 and 300,000. These new organizations were similar to the old organizations established during the 1790s and early 1820s. Their members represented skilled laborers and their issues were generally the same, including competition from cheap workers, closed shop matters, and better wages to provide a decent living for themselves and their families.

An important difference was the establishment of centralized or city federations. Between 1833 and 1836, such federations were founded in 13 American cities, including New York, Philadelphia, Boston, Albany, Pittsburgh, and Louisville. Many of these new organizations were coordinated through a new umbrella group, the National Trades Union (NTU), founded in 1834. Organizers made it clear what they intended to accomplish through the NTU, writing in the new organization's chief organ, *The Union*: "Our object in the formation of the Trades' Union was not to create a feeling of enmity against the non-producers . . . [but] to raise in the estimation of themselves and others, those who are the producers of the necessaries and luxuries of life."[32] For all its importance, the NTU did not last long, dissolving after only three years due to a new economic depression, the Panic of 1837.

BRINGING LEADERS TOGETHER

One of the most significant results of the organization of the NTU was to bring several of the leading labor organizers across the country together. For the first time, these leaders and their working-class followers had a sense of shared purpose. Among those who played key roles in NTU conventions over the following years, five labor leaders stood at the front: John Farrell, William English, Charles Douglas, Seth Luther, and Ely Moore.

Ely Moore served as the NTU's first president. Earlier in life, he had attended school as a medical student, but gave that field up to become a journeyman printer. He was "tall, handsome, with curly black hair brushed back over a broad forehead, invariably well dressed and habitually carrying an ivory-headed cane."[33] Early in his labor union career, Moore led the General Trades' Union in New York. An eloquent speaker, he was elected to Congress just as he was chosen as the leader of the NTU. In government, Moore was a spokesperson for America's organized workers.

Farrell, "the aggressive handloom weaver who led the successful ten-hour strike in Philadelphia,"[34] became an important voice at NTU conventions. He constantly spoke out in support of direct economic action by the labor unions, even as he warned members to beware of politicians who promised everything but produced little on behalf of the nation's organized workers. William English, another Philadelphia labor leader, was a journeyman

COMMITTEE OF ARBITRATION AT WORK.

During the 1830s and '40s, skilled laborers in 13 major U.S. cities organized city federations under the umbrella of the National Trades Union (NTU) to fight for workers' rights. One of the prominent organizers in Philadelphia was John Farrell, who organized a carpet weavers strike in Philadelphia in the 1830s, depicted here.

shoemaker, who was remembered for his fiery and impassioned speeches at NTU conventions and other labor gatherings.

Charles Douglas came into organized labor as one of the founders of the New England Association of Farmers, Mechanics, and Other Workingmen. He also worked as the editor of the labor publication the *New England Artisan*. One of Douglas's chief interests as a labor leader was his support of New England textile workers, many of whom were women. Like Farrell, Douglas also warned workers not to become entangled in politics.

Douglas was supported by another New England union leader, Seth Luther, who worked with him on the *New England Artisan* as a roving reporter of sorts and was known by the nickname the "Traveling Agent." He was, perhaps, one of the more colorful labor leaders, "a tall, lanky, tobacco-chewing Yankee, habitually wearing a bright green jacket, who toured through the factory towns calling upon the workers to defend their rights."[35] Through his writing, he publicized the plights of many women and children who labored under difficult conditions in New England's cotton mills. His words created clear pictures, meant to call to action those individuals who sought better lives for the working class: "While music floats from quivering strings through the perfumed and adorned apartments . . . of the rich, the nerves of the poor woman and child, in the cotton mills, are quivering with almost *dying agony*, from *excessive labor* to support this splendor."[36]

A WIDER TREND FOR THE MOVEMENT

The NTU and other new organizations took organized labor into uncharted waters—they published labor newspapers and provided a broader base of support for strikes, a forum for launching new unions, and a significant campaign platform for reform. The most important goal of the federations, however, was to ensure that the average workday was reduced from 12 hours to 10. The labor members held strike after strike to reduce their hours and even petitioned the federal government for legislation.

One of the most significant and largest of the federation strikes of the period was held in the summer of 1835 in Philadelphia, where the city's Trades Union brought workers together from 17 different crafts to give their support to Irish laborers who loaded and unloaded coal barges plying the Schuylkill River. It marked the first general strike in American history and was surprisingly successful. After three weeks of striking, Philadelphia's municipal leaders agreed to 10-hour days for city workers with no reduction in their pay. As a result, private companies and employers did the same thing. Soon, other union workers in Pennsylvania and neighboring states launched their own 10-hour work strikes and, by the fall of 1835, most had been successful.

The success of the National Trades Union was only one example of a new era of labor unrest among American workers. The NTU only included members who were skilled laborers. Following their example, unskilled workers established their own labor organizations during the 1830s and soon went out on strike, largely for better wages. This labor movement included significant numbers of women, including New York tailoresses, shoe binders from Philadelphia, and textile workers in Lowell, Massachusetts. During the summer of 1835, as Philadelphia found itself embroiled in a general strike of skilled workers, 500 unskilled female workers established a trade federation they called the Female Improvement Society. Through this organization, seamstresses sewing uniforms for the U.S. Army were granted higher wages.

Among unskilled male workers, Irish canal workers organized and became renowned for their militant behavior on behalf of their labor demands. Throughout the 1830s, Irish canal men organized 14 strikes, including one that led to a violent encounter between the canal workers and federal soldiers who were sent in to crush a strike called by workers on the Chesapeake and Ohio Canal in Maryland. The Irish were also at the center of labor disputes in New York City involving sailors, stevedores (those who carried freight onto and off ships), coal heavers, and construction workers.

With an ever-increasing threat of strikes and walkouts, American employers of the era were often frustrated, angry, and determined to fight their workers. Some employers fired workers who joined a labor organization and blacklisted them to make certain they did not get jobs elsewhere. Just as in earlier eras, court cases in the 1830s typically ruled that strikes and even the unions themselves were unlawful, violating conspiracy laws. When 20 New York journeymen tailors went to court and were found guilty of criminal conspiracy after they engaged in a strike against shops that did not recognize wage agreements, a mob of more than 25,000, more than one of every five people in the city, marched on city hall to protest the court's decision. Such decisions threatened the very lifeblood of the labor movement of the 1830s. The National Trades Union was uncertain of the movement's future following the tailors' conviction. Then, in 1837, another economic depression hit the country, dealing a near death blow to the NTU and to unions throughout the United States as wages fell and many were unemployed.

Support for the labor movement had at last found its way into national politics, however. Both the major political parties of the day—the Democrats and the Whigs—began to campaign actively for the vote of the average worker. In 1840, during his last full year in the White House, President Martin Van Buren helped pass legislation in the Congress establishing a 10-hour workday for workers engaged in federal construction projects. The new law was a shot in the arm to the NTU and other labor organizations and was

Martin Van Buren was one of the first presidents to support labor. In 1838, he became the first president to mediate a strike settlement, and two years later, he signed an executive order making the 10-hour workday mandatory for those workers who were engaged in federal construction projects.

followed just two years later by a court case in Massachusetts. The Whig-led state supreme court made a decision in the case *Commonwealth v. Hunt.*

The case was simple and straightforward. A labor organization, the Journeymen Bootmakers' Society of

Boston, had made a joint agreement among its members not to work for anyone who employed a journeyman who was not a member of their organization. The court's chief justice, Judge Lemuel Shaw, stated in his decision that "the manifest purpose of the society was to induce all those who engaged in the same occupation to become members, and that this could not be considered unlawful."[37] The refusal of the union's members to work for those who employed nonunion members did not, in the court's opinion, constitute a criminal act. Chief Justice Shaw compared the union members' refusal to work for employers hiring nonunion journeymen to a reform society whose members agree not to work for any employer who "employed a user of ardent spirits."[38] To Shaw, and to the Massachusetts court, such an agreement on behalf of a legal decision could not constitute conspiracy.

Unlike so many legal battles before, which often hampered the power and even the existence of labor unions in the United States, this decision established that workers had the right to organize strikes if the work stoppage was for "useful and honorable purposes."[39] On this point, though, the court's decision hung. In Judge Shaw's words, "The legality of such an association will . . . depend upon the means to be used for its accomplishment."[40]

For unions, the decision was an important step forward. Such organizations had finally won an element of legitimacy from the highest court in a state. From this point on, union organization in the United States and the principle of the closed shop had received significant support. The Massachusetts Supreme Court had not opened the flood gates on behalf of unionism in the United States, but it had opened a valve that would never again be closed.

4

A New Generation of Labor

By the 1840s, America's workers moved into a new era for labor and labor organizations. Nearly all of the labor federations founded during the 1830s had failed, brought down by the economic decline ushered in by the Panic of 1837. Even this new phase of organized labor continued to campaign for some of the earlier causes—especially the 10-hour workday. Workers across the country clamored for the reduction of work hours from 12 to 10, without a drop in their pay. There was no national labor organization spearheading the drive, but the "de facto headquarters"[41] of the campaign was the New England Workingmen's Association, established in 1844.

The name itself is somewhat misleading, for this labor organization included not only men in its ranks, but women as well, with the vast majority of both sexes working in New England's cotton textile mills. For this group, the goal of a 10-hour workday was only a portion of its agenda, which called for a new social structure. Leaders of the organization believed that, once its members gained the 10-hour workday, they would have more personal time available to become involved in the pervasive reform movements that were sweeping the country during the 1840s. Reformers were calling for the abolition of slavery; changes in America's prisons; the destruction of state gambling lotteries; humanitarian treatment of the insane; the establishment of free, public education; the elimination of prostitution; women's rights; and other measures to bring about improvements in American society. The 10-hour workday would allow workers to "take the business of reform into [their] own hands" and allow them to join the campaigns against "the general evils of social life as it is."[42]

In general, during the 1840s and 1850s, the fight to work only 10 hours per day would be fought using political means. Workers drew up petitions and beat the streets to pressure state legislators to draw up laws prohibiting industrial employers from working anyone more than 10 hours a day. Some responded positively. A 10-hour law was passed in New Hampshire in 1847 and in Pennsylvania and Maine the following year. Six additional states—Connecticut, Ohio, Georgia, New Jersey, Rhode Island, and California, newly admitted to the Union as a state in 1850—passed similar laws throughout the 1850s. Many of these laws were unenforceable or ineffective because of a variety of loopholes built into the original legislation. Such loopholes allowed for "special contracts" that allowed for more than 10 hours of labor a day, and such agreements between employers and workers were not uncommon. Despite the New England Workingmen's Association, the Massachusetts legislature refused to pass a 10-hour workday law, because of the power of the state's textile mill owners.

Although the 10-hour workday was a main issue of the 1840s, other issues were also important to some workers. One of the best examples of a labor organization that gave support to a broader agenda than just the number of hours in the workday was the Lowell Female Labor Reform Association (LFLRA). The Lowell textile mills in Massachusetts employed women almost exclusively, making the LFLRA the largest women's union within the umbrella organization of the New

England Workingmen's Association. These working women supported reforms (such as the temperance movement) that sought the prohibition of alcohol and the abolition of capital punishment and slavery, even as they sought the recognition of women's rights. Lowell workers had even formed a female antislavery society as early as 1832.

REORGANIZATION AND FRAGMENTATION

The 1840s introduced other new labor organizations that began to dot the landscape of the American working class. There would be many new single trade unions for workers who worked in every field of skilled labor, from construction workers to typesetters to cigar makers. Many of these union groups were established on a local level, with no national intentions. Sometimes local labor organizations were established by criteria other than just the type of labor its members were trained to do. Some labor organizations of this era were also based on sex, nationality, or race of its members. There were black labor groups and ethnic immigrant groups. Many workingmen's groups did not allow for women members, so female workers involved in that type of labor organized their own labor groups.

The Lowell Female Labor Reform Association was one such organization. In its literature, female members were reminded: "You have been degraded long enough. Resolve that you will think, reason, judge, love, hate, approve and disapprove, for yourselves, and at your own volition; and, not at the dictation of another."[43] One of the Lowell Association's rallying cries became, "Equal rights or death to the corporations."[44]

Such slogans as this helped the goals of the working women of New England to dovetail with another women's movement of the 1840s, the campaign for women's equal rights. In the summer of 1848, the first national women's rights convention was held at Seneca Falls, New York. Although the Lowell Association did not send anyone to represent its workers directly at the convention, there were working women present, including Charlotte Woodward, a 19-year-old seamstress who lived in Seneca County, who sewed deerskin gloves. Her dream was to become a typesetter, but no printer would take on a woman as an apprentice or journeyman. Years later, she would write of her frustration: "I wanted to work, but I wanted to choose my task. . . . That was my form of rebellion against the life into which I was born."[45] Before she left the Seneca Falls convention, young Woodward would sign her name to the document drawn up by those in attendance, a Declaration of Principles patterned after the Declaration of Independence. The rewording: "We hold these truths to be self evident: that all men and women are created equal."[46] But even as the laboring women of America were actively seeking their equal rights, a sad reality was true: Many of the labor unions across the country did not even allow women to be members.

THE IMPACT OF IMMIGRATION

As labor found new goals to place alongside earlier, yet unfulfilled, causes, the 1840s would prove to be a difficult decade for organized workers in the United States. It was during that decade, stretching into the 1850s, that the country would become the destination of a seemingly countless number of foreign immigrants. The sheer numbers were staggering. Between the founding of the United States during the 1770s and the following half century, about 1 million immigrants reached American shores to make the young republic their home. During just one decade—1846 to 1855—however, the total number of new immigrants would be an additional 3 million.

(continues on page 58)

THE LOWELL GIRLS

Few causes spurred the early unionization movement in the United States more than that of low wages for both skilled and unskilled workers. Another issue was often on the minds of those who banded together in the labor organizations of the late 1700s and early 1800s, however—working conditions. Poor conditions were a common circumstance of the Industrial Revolution, which began in England. Those who invested in the first full-blown factories, production mills, and plants spent little money making their workplaces safe, much less pleasant, for their workers. Several American capitalists in Massachusetts, however, when establishing some of the first factories in the United States, tried to accomplish both aims. Their textile mills would revolve around a system of labor that would be known as the Lowell System. At its heart were its workers, nearly all of whom were young, single women. By making their factories acceptable places to work, the Lowell Manufacturing Company was able to attract the kinds of workers they wanted, not the kind for which they might have to settle.

When these early textile facilities went online in Massachusetts, the developers relied on local labor—New England farm girls—who had few job opportunities. These first factory developers "wanted to prevent the oppression of the workers that had so notoriously resulted from the development of the factory system abroad."* The concept of the Lowell System (also known as the Waltham System, for textile factories built in Waltham, Massachusetts) was not only to employ young, single women, but to provide them a homelike atmosphere, a female boarding school of sorts, where the women would be employed rather than attend classes.

Although most factories did little to make work tolerable for their workers, the Lowell organizers did as much as possible to make the workplace pleasant. The women who worked at these special plants were treated fairly, and their health was protected by an acceptable work environment. The factory owners even felt responsible for the morality of their female workers. The girls first had to leave their farming homes and move to the factory where they were assigned quarters in several factory-owned boardinghouses. There, they were watched closely, often by specially assigned older women, and had to live by rules designed to guard their personal lives. The girls were expected to be in their rooms by 10 P.M., and church attendance was mandatory. Any girl found guilty of immodesty, profanity, or dancing was fired. More serious moral lapses had the same results. According to the guidelines established by the Lowell Manufacturing Company concerning its male employees, the organization would not "continue to employ any person who shall be wanting in proper respect to the females employed by the company, or who shall smoke within the company's premises, or be guilty of inebriety."**

Despite the positive work environment and living conditions established by the Lowell Company, its workers were expected to put in long hours on the job (about 11 to 12 daily). This was not as difficult or harsh as it might appear, since many of the female laborers worked at the company looms, which, as factory work went at that time, was not particularly difficult or exacting labor. The young female workers were provided with regular breaks during the workday when they might read or have a pleasant conversation with fellow workers.

Although the working men and women of the Lowell plants were expected to pay for their room and board out of their earnings, they usually had money left over, typically $2 per week. By today's standards, this seems like a small amount, but "for members of farm families for whom any cash income was almost unknown, even this small sum seemed like riches."*** Often, the girls put their extra cash in local banks, and it was not uncommon for Lowell workers to have as much as $500 on deposit.

Despite the positive elements of the Lowell System, many of the girls who worked in these factories were not employed for long. The vast majority worked for only a few years, just enough time to save money for a marriage or to get another job, often that of schoolteacher. In addition, these women workers rarely came to feel any sense of commitment to the Lowell Company. They could and did leave at any time they chose, and, typically, many of the girls were laid off during less

(continues)

(continued)

productive months, returning home to their family farms for lengthy breaks.

In time, the idealistic relationship between the employers and employees of the Lowell Manufacturing System experienced negative change. As competition between factories increased, the kinder, gentler approach to employing young girls took a backseat to productivity. Instead, mill owners reduced wages, enforced longer hours, and then stepped up the pace of the work. By the late 1840s, where one female worker had been in charge of a pair of looms during an average work-day during the previous decade, the number of looms had been increased to four. Competition and productivity at all costs became the new watchword, even in the Lowell textile mills. As one manager said of his workers, "I regard my work-people just as I regard my machinery. So long as they can do my work for what I choose to pay them, I keep them, getting out of them all I can."[†] Such a comment makes clear how far the Lowell System, once a grand example of cooperation and benevolence between employer and employee, had declined, all in the name of profit.

---

* Foster Rhea Dulles and Melvyn Dubofsky, *Labor in America: A History* (Arlington Heights, Ill.: Harlan Davidson, 1984), 74.

** Ibid.

*** Ibid.

† Ibid., 75.

(continued from page 55)

A prolonged potato famine in Ireland forced many Irish to leave their island homeland and take up residence in the United States. Because of their abject poverty, many of these new arrivals to America did not fan out across the country. Once they landed in an East Coast port, they generally stayed put, making their new homes in cities from Boston to New York. The vast majority of these new arrivals were not only poor, but also unskilled and untrained laborers, ready to work for any wage, no matter how low. Any regular wage would be better than what had been their way of life back in Ireland. The effect of immigration on the labor movement of the 1840s and 1850s was largely negative.

The 1850s was not a total loss for labor, however. Labor organizations were established throughout the decade. A brief depression in 1857 caused some setbacks, but the overall impact of the 1850s was that the unions were "less concerned over the solidarity of labor and fastened their attention far more narrowly on the needs of their own individual membership."[47] As in earlier decades, the general movement was in support of skilled craftsmen who worked

During the 1840s, a prolonged potato famine in Ireland forced many Irish to immigrate to the United States in search of better opportunities. This new influx of unskilled laborers hurt the labor movement because these new immigrants would often work longer hours for lower wages.

the old, established trades. One group whose needs were not addressed during the movement of the 1850s, generally speaking, was that of the unskilled worker. The gap between skilled and unskilled widened as the skilled workers "became reluctant to link their fortunes to the [unskilled]."[48]

LABOR DURING THE CIVIL WAR

Much of this development and division between the unskilled and skilled workers would be lost during the Civil War. Events had been pushing the nation closer to war for decades, the issue generally being the expansion of slavery into the western territories and states. Many of the leading labor organizations, for the most part having developed in northern cities, supported some compromise between the two sides threatening war. Members of 34 of the most important unions agreed to work together in early 1861 as a show of force against the separated halves of the country, their common slogan being, "Concession not Secession."[49]

Even before the first shots of the war were fired and following the secession of several Southern states from the Union, a National Workingmen's Convention was held in February 1861, in Philadelphia. The position of workers concerning the divided country and the movement toward war was clear. Those in attendance issued a statement that read, "Under the leadership of political demagogues and traitors, the country is going to the devil as fast as it can, and unless the masses rise up in their might, and teach their representatives what to do, the good old ship will go to pieces."[50]

When the war began in the spring of 1861, the nation officially divided into North and South, and so did the labor movement. Many Northern workers sided with President Lincoln and the Union, believing that the Republican Party's ideals more closely fit the agenda of the labor movement. Some Republicans, at least, saw the war as a "struggle between freedom and slavery, democracy and aristocracy, equality and privilege,"[51] which made the struggle of the nation sound much like the struggle of the labor movement itself.

At first, the war proved to be a hardship on the American labor movement. Workers were drafted into military service, whereas the wealthy only had to pay $400 to avoid military duty. Wartime inflation spiked the cost of living, especially for the poor. The war also proved to be a positive for the labor movement, however. With the government purchasing massive quantities of manufactured goods and creating an increased market for raw materials, including everything needed to fight a war—iron, steel, gunpowder, lumber, coal—manufacturers were making a lot of money. With this, the trickle down impacted the workingman. Labor gained strength and a new voice as the war continued over the next four years.

Between 1863 and 1864, the number of trade unions increased from 79 to an unprecedented 270, with a total membership of 200,000 organized workers. Among these, 32 unions were national in scope. Organized groups that led the pack included the Iron Molders' International Union, as well as trade organizations uniting machinists, blacksmiths, locomotive engineers, miners, and ironworkers. There were occasional criticisms when labor organizations went out on strike during the war for higher wages and other causes, but, overall, President Lincoln was prolabor. "Thank God we have a system of labor where there can be a strike," Lincoln once stated, and he remained positive about organized labor throughout the bloody national conflict.[52] By the end of the war, the American labor movement was ready to advance itself even further. One of the most important directions taken that next year was on behalf of the establishment of the National Labor Union.

FOUNDING THE NATIONAL LABOR UNION

From its founding, the National Labor Union (NLU) was intended to mirror labor's expectations of progress after the Civil War—to take the movement in a new direction, one more radical than ever before. The NLU was established in Baltimore at a labor convention in 1866. As with earlier organizations, this one brought together laborers in a variety of work fields, including metal workers, coal miners, shoemakers and clothing workers, and typesetters and typographers. The new group's agenda gave support to a wide variety of causes and goals, including the mandate by state law of an eight-hour workday (by the mid-1860s, some had not yet institutionalized the 10-hour workday). The NLU also supported banking and currency reform; fair tax codes; an end to contracting prison labor; the Homestead Act, which distributed western federal lands; and the formation of a National Labor Party.

The NLU's founder was a tough ironworker named William Sylvis. Sylvis was born in 1828, one of a dozen siblings whose father was a Pennsylvania wagon maker. At age 18, Sylvis was apprenticed to a local iron plant. In 1855, he moved to Philadelphia to work and joined the Stove Molders' Union. In a short time, he became one of the organization's most important leaders. Four years after joining, he helped establish the National Molders' Union, but the organization fell apart with the outbreak of the Civil War. Many of the group's members, including Sylvis, joined the Union Army to fight the Confederacy. In 1863, when his service to his country was completed, Sylvis returned home and rejoined the National Molders' Union, becoming the organization's president.

Sylvis was a dedicated and seemingly tireless labor organizer. He traveled across the country, organizing molders, even as he lived on the donations he received from each local union organization. In time, the molders' union became one of the most powerful and influential in the nation. Through his efforts and insight, the National Labor Union was established. He kept at his work as a labor organizer until 1869, when he died suddenly just before the 1869 NLU convention.

His support for the labor movement would be Sylvis's legacy. His commitment to labor rang clear through his life, as both his deeds and words reflect. Sylvis was a man of strong conviction and equally strong opinions, such as his views of those who owned the means of production and of workers themselves:

> Capital blights and withers all it touches. It is a new aristocracy, proud, imperious, dishonest, seeking only profit and exploitation of the workers [while] labor is the foundation of the entire political, social and commercial structure . . . the attribute of all that is noble and good in civilization. . . . Let our cry be REFORM. . . . Down with a monied aristocracy and up with the people.[53]

Few labor organizations of this period in American history were as open in their acceptance of a wide range of workers as the NLU. Women's labor organizations were allowed to join the NLU, including the Daughters of St. Crispin, a union of female shoemakers, the first national union of women working in industry. It was at an annual NLU convention that an endorsement was made to push for equity in pay between men and women. As the organization's statement boldly expressed, the NLU hoped to encourage employers to "do justice to women by paying them equal wages for equal work."[54]

The NLU was open to a wide variety of workers. Unlike other labor organizations, the National Labor Union endorsed the organization of black workers. Blacks were allowed to attend the national NLU conventions as early as 1869. Before the year's end, Isaac Myers, the leader of the Colored Caulkers' Trade Union Society in Baltimore, formed the Colored National Labor Union (CNLU). Despite its openness in accepting women and blacks, the organization did have its limits. Unlike other groups at the time whose members advocated voting rights for women, the NLU did not. Also, the NLU sought to have Chinese immigration to America cut off; it believed that Chinese workers undercut American laborers by accepting low wages.

Despite the initial success of the NLU, the organization took serious hits during the Panic of 1873. Yet another economic depression in the United States caused serious business downturns, with as many as 5,000 businesses failing. High unemployment was the order of the day, and unions found it difficult to hold the line on wages. Many unions across the United States were crushed. In 1870, before the depression hit, there were approximately 30 national labor organizations representing 300,000 workers. By 1877, only nine national labor organizations were still intact, and the number of union members had been reduced to only 50,000, a fraction of the millions of workers in the United States. With the effects of the Panic of 1873 still ongoing that year, "only one-fifth of the labor force had steady, full-time jobs."[55]

With labor organizations reeling and struggling to survive, employers and sometimes government officials made attempts to cause further damage to their workers' unions. When labor activists held a rally in New York City during

After the Panic of 1873, the resulting depression caused many Americans to protest the loss of jobs and the influx of immigrants who they believed were taking their jobs. Here, members of the New York militia fire on a crowd of anti-Irish demonstrators in New York City in 1877.

the winter of 1873–1874, thousands of men and women demonstrated in Tompkins Square on the city's Lower East Side, one of the poorest parts of New York. The city dispatched police to the scene, "who charged into the Square without warning, clubbing right and left as mounted officers chased down people fleeing through the side streets."[56] Hundreds of poor, hungry laborers were injured and arrested. In Pennsylvania, when labor leaders tried to put pressure on the Philadelphia and Reading Railroad by organizing a strike of anthracite coal miners in 1875, the railroad first went to court, then hired agents of the Pinkerton Detective Agency to infiltrate a group of Irish miners known as the "Molly Maguires," which resulted in false accusations against the miners and led to their arrests and convictions for murder. Nineteen Irish miners were hanged by the summer of 1877. Labor leaders organized the Great Railroad Strike of 1877, which was soon crushed when government officials aided railroad companies by dispatching state militia troops to put down the strikers. Worker-militia violence in Pittsburgh on July 20 led to the deaths of nearly four dozen workers, even as 500 railroad cars, more than 100 locomotives, and nearly 40 buildings were destroyed.

The Panic of 1873 brought utter destruction to the labor movement, bringing a close to the new era of labor organization that had followed the Civil War. The "democratic revolution"[57] of the labor movement was over. Labor unions were certainly not dead, but the movement would take a new direction in the following decades. America itself was headed into a new era, one that would one day be referred to as the Gilded Age. It would span 25 years, taking the nation straight into a new century. The new age would feature the efforts of America's new barons of industry, great organizers who built larger and larger factories and mills, forging steel and iron, founding new railroads and steamship companies, creating "glittering riches for American capitalists and leaden poverty for masses of working people."[58] For labor organizers across the United States, the Gilded Age would present greater challenges than ever before.

5

The Knights of Labor

The Gilded Age would be an age of change, progress, diversification, productivity, and riches. The Civil War served as its first catalyst, creating the need for vast amounts of war equipment and raw materials, to supply the giant armies, especially that of the North, to fight a war that would involve a total of 3 million men in arms. The two generations that followed, taking the United States from the end of the Civil War to the end of the nineteenth century, would continue the trend toward massive manufacturing and greater industrialization. The time would be one of dazzling economic expansion and progress never before witnessed in the American republic. The growth could be found in every facet of American production:

> The railroads flung out new networks of rails to span the continent and knit the country into an economic whole. The burning stacks of steel mills lighting the skies over Pittsburgh symbolized the growth of gigantic industry made possible by the discovery of the incalculable iron resources of the Mesabi Range in Minnesota. Oil gushed from wells in western Pennsylvania and Ohio. In the great slaughterhouses of Chicago, Cincinnati, and St. Louis, thousands of cattle and hogs were butchered daily. The textile mills of New England hummed with activity and a ready-made clothing industry grew up out of the sweatshops of New York and other eastern cities. Everywhere new factories

and mills reflected the triumphs of the machine and the growth of mass production. As cities and manufacturing towns mushroomed along the Atlantic seaboard and in the Middle West, the face of America was transformed.59

This new era dawned because all the elements needed for a new industrial revolution in the United States were finally solidly in place. The country's vast natural resources were being tapped, new markets were making greater demands on production than ever before, and the country had a vast reservoir of labor. At the helm of this mammoth economic development were the capitalists, entrepreneurs destined for America's history books. They included railroaders, such as Jay Gould, E. H. Harriman, and James J. Hill; Scottish immigrant Andrew Carnegie and his steel empire; and John D. Rockefeller and his giant oil company. These barons of a new era of American production were only limited by their visions and their ethics. The companies and corporations they founded and built were national organizations, many of them models of monopoly, cornering the market on the production of everything from sugar to oil, steel to lumber.

As these tycoons of industry expanded their various empires, they carried the working men and women of the United States along with them. As historian Edward Bellamy would write:

> Before this concentration began . . . the individual workman was relatively important and independent in his relations to the employer. . . . Labor unions were needless then and general strikes out of the question. But when the era of small concerns with small capital was succeeded by that of the great aggregations of capital, all this was changed. The individual laborer . . . was reduced to insignificance and powerlessness against the great corporation. . . . Self-defense drove him to union with his fellows.60

American capitalists such as Jay Gould, who built his fortune through the development and speculation of railroads, followed a policy of the "iron law of wages." This practice espoused paying employees the lowest possible wage they would accept, which was made easier by the influx of immigrants.

The new captains of industry would use every tool at their disposal to reduce the power of labor unions over their operations. The rule of thumb was the "iron law of wages." Employers would pay wages as low as any workforce would accept. As millions of new immigrants made their way to the United States during the 1880s and 1890s, it became more difficult for labor unions to hold the line on wages. Supply and demand was having a direct impact on the amount of money large companies were willing to pay their workers. In addition, the up-and-down economy of this era wreaked havoc on laborers, organized or not. The Panic of 1873 did not wind down until 1878 and was followed by another short-lived recession between 1883 and 1885. A widespread depression hit the country hard between 1893 and 1897. These downturns forced workers to accept wage cuts and caused high unemployment.

To make matters worse, the government itself seemed to conspire against the working persons. Many government leaders, including U.S. presidents and members of Congress, had ties with big business and counted them as their chief supporters and friends. Little federal legislation that was friendly to labor was passed during the last two or three decades of the nineteenth century.

Then, in 1886, the U.S. Supreme Court handed down a ruling that American corporations were protected under the Fourteenth Amendment, just as were American citizens. Laws—both federal and state—that had been positive for labor were soon nullified; they included those limiting labor hours and establishing minimum wages. Judges across the country seemed to turn against organized labor, often issuing injunctions against such labor organization and union actions as strikes, boycotts, and other public demonstrations against their employers.

The new capitalists seemed to take control of America's economic system and its directions, and labor took a back-seat. Those in economic power cared little for the working class. As Jay Gould, who amassed a fortune in railroads and steamships, as well as controlling interest in the Western Union Telegraph Company, stated coldly of America's workers: "I can hire one-half of the working class to kill the other half."[61]

LABOR FIGHTS BACK

Even as America's capitalists tried to squash the power of the workers, they were inadvertently giving them new power—through sheer numbers. As the industrial giants nurtured and expanded their businesses, factories, mills, companies, and corporations, they needed more and more workers. The numbers were highly significant. In 1870, the number of wageworkers stood at about 6.7 million. By 1900, however, wage earners numbered about 18 million. When one considered their families, these workers "added up to at least three-quarters of the U.S. population of 76 million."[62]

In addition, many of the era's working class were made up of immigrants, recent arrivals to the United States. From 1873 through the following quarter century, 10 million new immigrants reached America's shores and entered the workforce. Many counted in this new generation of immigrants came from central and eastern Europe, including Italy, Austria-Hungary, Russia, Greece, and Poland. Others arrived from the Middle East, Japan, China, the Caribbean, South America, and Mexico. They left their homes in the Old Country to find work and a new livelihood in the United States. Large numbers of workers from the same countries took jobs in the same fields. Eastern Europeans took work as miners, steelworkers, and members of railroad maintenance crews. Italians and Russians, many of whom were Jewish, went into the garment industry. Latin Americans worked making cigars. This new melting pot of workers did not always find jobs of their choice, however. Some struggled to find work at all.

A NEW LABOR ORGANIZATION

The new labor movement of the Gilded Age approached this new mix and great expanse of workers and saw a new future for organized labor. Throughout the 1880s and 1890s, labor fought ferociously for its goals. During those years, labor organizations sponsored more than 18,000 strikes across the country; these work stoppages were on behalf of better pay, union recognition, and the eight-hour day, a relatively new goal. Emerging as a new leader among the labor organizations of this era was one established in the early years of the Gilded Age—the Noble and Holy Order of the Knights of Labor. This labor body was founded in 1869 by a group of garment workers, led by a Philadelphia tailor named Uriah Stephens. Stephens led the Knights of Labor for a decade until he stepped down. He was replaced by "a mild and dapper little Irish mechanic,"[63] Terrence Powderly, in 1879, when he was already serving as the mayor of Scranton, Pennsylvania.

During the organization's early years, from 1869 until 1881, the Knights remained a secret organization, to avoid having its members blacklisted by their employers. Complicated codes were created to inform members of scheduled meetings. Coded messages might be chalked on factory walls to inform the members of a particular "trade assembly" of the time to meet. At the heart of the Knights' mission was a keen sense of solidarity among its members and their various craft and trade organizations. The Knights' motto: "An Injury to One is an Injury to All."[64]

Once the Knights of Labor became strong and confident enough, the labor group went public in 1881. In doing so, the organization's leaders issued a public statement called a Declaration of Principles. The mission statement was clearly worded:

> The alarming development and aggressiveness of great capitalists and corporations, unless checked, will inevitably lead to the pauperization and hopeless degradation of the toiling masses. . . . It is imperative . . . that a check be placed upon unjust accumulation, and the power for evil of

In 1869, Philadelphia tailor Uriah Stephens helped found the Knights of Labor, the first national labor union in the United States. Stephens served as leader of the Knights until he stepped down after an unsuccessful congressional bid in 1878.

aggregated wealth.... This ... can be accomplished only by the united efforts of those who obey the divine injunction, "In the sweat of thy face shalt thou eat bread."[65]

Members of the Knights created their own special brand of labor organizing. Its members sought arbitration of disagreements between employers and workers, rather than strikes and work stoppages. They sought the eight-hour workday, and they were opposed to contract labor and convict labor, as well as to child labor. Its members wanted

(continues on page 76)

STEPHENS, SECRECY, AND SPECIAL SIGNS

With the death of William Sylvis in 1869, the collapse of the National Labor Union was inevitable, leaving a gaping hole in the movement to organize America's working class. Before year's end, however, another labor organization was founded, in Sylvis's own home city—Philadelphia. There, a handful of well-intentioned garment workers established the Noble and Holy Order of the Knights of Labor. The intention of the garment cutters was to establish a better labor organization, "something that will be different from what we have ever had."* Its first leader would make certain that the Knights of Labor was just that—different.

Uriah S. Stephens, the leader of the Knights, had been a member of Philadelphia's Garment Cutters Association. The Association was dead, though, and the Knights represented the new order, one that Stephens took seriously from the beginning. His background only helped prepare him for his new role. He was born to Quaker parents in the town of Cape May, New Jersey, on August 3, 1821. As a teen, he became convinced of a call to the Baptist ministry. But he was forced to drop his religious studies during the Panic of 1837 and become an apprentice to a tailor in Philadelphia. By 1845, he left the city and struck out on his own to make a living in his new trade. Finding little fulfillment as a tailor, he sought adventure in the early 1850s, when he went West to California to prospect for gold in the Great Rush. Failing to make his fortune in the gold camps, Stephens moved back to Philadelphia in 1858, where he spoke out publicly in favor of abolitionism, a reform movement seeking an end to slavery in America. Stephens was also involved in other organizations, as well. He was a Freemason, an Odd Fellow, a Knight of Pythias—all secret fraternal orders.

Having returned to the tailoring business in Philadelphia, Stephens soon became involved with the labor movement, helping to organize the Garment Cutters Association. Through the short years of the group's existence, Stephens learned several lessons about how to create a successful labor organization. His first lesson was that single trade unions were generally too small and isolated from other unions to accomplish much. His second insight was that capitalism, by design,

would always naturally oppress the working class. In the aftermath of the failed Garment Cutters Association, Stephens and several other tailors and garment workers established a new labor group, the Knights of Labor. The group drew up a mission statement that included accepting other types of laborers into their organization and to bring down the wage system they felt was so unfair.

Although the Knights were open to "all branches of honorable toil,"** Stephens's religious background and his love for secret societies helped impact the organization. For one, all those wishing to join the Knights first had to answer three questions positively: (1) Do you believe in God, the Creator and Father of All? (2) Do you obey the Universal ordinance of God, in gaining your bread by the sweat of your brow? (3) Are you willing to take a solemn vow binding you to secrecy, obedience, and mutual assistance?***

The importance Stephens placed on secrecy was essential to him, because he thought it would help protect members from employers and labor spies. He created secret rituals, and a special sign and password only to be used among the Knights themselves. In fact, Stephens was so attached to secrecy that for the first dozen years of the organization's existence, the Knights of Labor was only referred to in writing as five asterisks. Thus, a secret meeting of the Knights might be announced with a message chalked on a wall reading "***** 8 610/75." To members in the know, this would translate as, "Knights will meet at 8 P.M. on June 10 at Assembly 75." Stephens was one of the originators of such secret codes and procedures, but these safeguards did not end with him. After 10 years as the leader of the Knights, he was replaced by Terence Powderly, who decided the secret rituals and signals were too important to the organization's safety to abandon.

---

* Charles A. Madison, *American Labor Leaders: Personalities and Forces in the Labor Movement* (New York: Frederick Ungar, 1960), 44.
** Ibid., 45.
*** Ibid.

(continued from page 73)

healthy work conditions and new codes and regulations to make factories, mills, and mines safer. They also supported the idea of equal pay for men and women, for equal work accomplished.

The Knights of Labor poured much effort into organizing many local labor assemblies, which admitted both skilled and unskilled workers. Those unskilled workers of the 1880s could not really be ignored, because they made up 70 percent or so of the nation's labor force. The Knights also organized black labor assemblies, and the labor group allowed women to join by 1882, following the organizing of women shoe workers in Philadelphia. Immigrants, often shunned by other labor groups, were also admitted to the Knights. Although some western-based Knights fought Chinese membership, Knights chapters in New York and Philadelphia tried to organize Chinese workers. The Knights eventually allowed membership to include groups of the "producing classes," who were not wage earners, such as farmers, ministers, shop owners, doctors, writers, publishers, editors, and even housewives. (The only worker groups not allowed membership with the Knights of Labor were liquor dealers, stockbrokers, bankers, corporate lawyers, and professional gamblers.)

With such broad membership, the Knights of Labor grew dramatically over the years. In 1880, while it was still a secret organization, the Knights numbered around 20,000 members. By 1882, membership was 43,000, and two years later, the Knights had grown to 71,000 members. The following year, the organization had 110,000 members. The growth over the next year was exponential—reaching an impressive three-quarters of a million. By then, local Knights organizations spanned the country, numbering 15,000. The Knights were almost everywhere in America, with only 70 counties in the country not having a Knights organization of some sort. By the mid-1880s, the labor organization had gone international, with groups in Canada, Great Britain, Ireland, Belgium, France, Italy, Australia, and New Zealand. The Knights of Labor had become "the most inclusive U.S. labor organization of the nineteenth century."[66]

The Knights of Labor was so uniquely structured that its operations spanned a wide variety of goals and efforts. The organization ran education programs and sponsored social events. They supported hundreds of candidates as they ran for political office during the mid-1880s. The Knights ran cooperatives to provide cheaper goods to members, bypassing the normal retail stores and businesses. At the heart of the Knights of Labor were the organized unions themselves.

Although early organizers tried to avoid strikes (Terence Powderly was always proud that the Knights did not strike while he was president of the organization), strikes did become a way of life for the labor organization. Many of the strikes that occurred during the mid-1880s were due to sympathy strikes that were called to support a strike by another labor group within the Knights organization. From California to New England, the Knights of Labor averaged about 450 strikes annually between 1881 and 1884. Larger numbers of strikes occurred during the mid-to-late 1880s, however, including 645 strikes in 1885 and more than 1,400 in both 1886 and 1887, respectively. The 1885 strikes were so successful that railroad tycoon Jay Gould gave in and rescinded 10 percent wage cuts he had put in place, which had led to the strikes in the first place.

FACING DOWN JAY GOULD

The year 1885 would be among the most momentous in the history of the Knights of Labor. Among the hundreds of strikes the Knights supported that year, one had the greatest impact.

Uriah Stephens's successor as leader of the Knights of Labor was Terence V. Powderly. The son of Irish immigrants, Powderly championed an eight-hour workday and served as the mayor of Scranton, Pennsylvania, from 1878 to 1884.

Ironically, it sprang from a labor campaign organized three years earlier, outside the Knights organization. In the fall of 1882, the Federation of Organized Trades and Labor Unions (FOTLU) was a small collective of national craft unions with no connection to the Knights of Labor. That September, FOTLU carried out a "labor holiday" parade, which consisted of 30,000 laborers—men and women alike—marching for their rights instead of going to their regular jobs. This march became the impetus for Labor Day, which, in 1894, became a national holiday. Other parades were staged during the following years in other cities, including Buffalo and Cincinnati. The main rallying cry was in favor of the eight-hour work day. Marchers regularly carried banners reading: "Eight Hours for Work, Eight Hours for Sleep, Eight Hours for What We Will."[67] During the 1884 FOTLU convention, the members in attendance voted officially that "eight hours shall constitute a legal day's labor from and after May 1, 1886."[68] If employers did not recognize this by that date, the FOTLU intended to call for a national work stoppage, hoping that other labor organizations would join them.

As for the Knights of Labor, its leader, Terence Powderly, and the organization's General Executive Board, did not back the stance and ultimatum handed down by the FOTLU. Despite this situation, street-level membership within the Knights favored the resolution, and many local Knights' chapters declared their support. Consequently, despite a lack of support from the top, membership in the Knights' organization increased seven times over between 1885 and 1886.

The movement to demand the eight-hour workday proved so inspirational to the Knights that the organization decided to challenge, once again, the notorious railroad tycoon Jay Gould to another showdown. Having already forced Gould to agree to rescind wage cuts the previous year, the Knights now set their sights on the railroad magnate. In February, Knights' members who worked on several of Gould's rail lines went out on strike, demanding that the railroad owner recognize union membership for all his workers who aligned themselves with a labor organization.

Gould came out swinging, sending in hired law enforcement officials to break the strike. Clashes in East St.

Louis resulted in the deaths of seven workers after they faced off with Illinois militiamen and police. After two months of the strike, it appeared that Gould was going to succeed in destroying the strikers. The Knights continued to force Gould's hand, however, as membership in the organization continued to grow. As one witness remarked, "Never has there been such a spectacle as the march of the Order of the Knights of Labor at the present time."[69]

The issues all converged in events that took place in Chicago on May 1. That day, a Saturday, about 350,000 workers representing the labor force at 11,000 businesses nationwide struck, demanding the implementation of the eight-hour workday. In Chicago alone, 65,000 workers participated in the strike, organizing rallies and labor parades. That Monday, employers responded, as police descended on the McCormick Harvesting Machine Company outside the city, to break up the strike, resulting in the deaths of four workers. The next day, May 4, supporters of the eight-hour work day called for a massive demonstration for that evening, to be held at Chicago's Haymarket Square. Although thousands did show up at the planned event, the number had fallen to several hundred by 10 P.M., when police showed up to send the crowd home.

Just after the arrival of the law enforcement officials, after 10:00 P.M., an unknown person tossed a bomb into a group of policemen and demonstrators, killing a police officer and wounding 66 other people, 7 of them dying later from their injuries. No one ever knew who threw the bomb or even why. Some of those who had organized the demonstration at the Haymarket that evening were members of an anarchist group that supported the eight-hour workday, but no direct connections to them were ever made. During the weeks that followed the Haymarket bombing, police arrested hundreds of labor organizers. Labor meetings were raided. During some of those raids, "evidence of incendiary plotting was seized—and planted when it could not be found."[70]

Before the end of the month, eight alleged anarchists—August Spies, Albert Parsons, Adolph Fischer, George Engel, Louis Lingg, Samuel Fielden, Oscar Neebe, and Michael Schwab—were placed on trial following their indictments based on charges of conspiracy to commit murder. The trial opened on June 21. During the trial, the evidence presented showed that only two of the eight men—Spies and Fielden—were present at the Haymarket when the bomb exploded.

The issue of who tossed the explosive device was secondary to the prosecutors, however. The accused were socialists, anarchists, radicals. The words of the prosecution tell the story: "Law is on trial. Anarchy is on trial. . . . Gentlemen of the jury: convict these men, make examples of them, hang them and you save our institutions, our society."[71] The jury heard the state's message and found all eight defendants guilty. One was sentenced to 15 years in prison; the other seven received the death penalty. During the intervening months, the governor of Illinois commuted the sentences of two of the convicted to life terms. A third condemned man committed suicide. The remaining four—Spies, Parsons, Fischer, and Engel—were hanged. An estimated crowd of 25,000 supporters and mourners marched in their funeral processions.

The violence in the Haymarket had claimed lives that day in May, as well as other lives, of those convicted of crimes they may or may not have committed. The Knights of Labor may have been a victim. In the aftermath of the labor conflicts at the McCormick Harvesting Machine Company and associated clashes between strikers and police, the campaign in support of an eight-hour workday died, and the prestige of the Knights began to fail. (Powderly himself turned conservative after the Haymarket incident, and he and the Knights General Executive Board would not even donate monies to the defense fund of the eight accused.) A series of labor disputes over the following year ended with the workers losing ground, further splitting the ranks of the Knights. Between 1886 and 1888, Knights membership tumbled from 750,000 to 220,000. Two years later, the Knights only numbered 100,000. By 1896, only 20,000 workers still allied themselves with the Knights of Labor.

6

The American Federation of Labor

The decline of the Knights of Labor paralleled the founding and advancement of yet another powerful and influential labor organization in the United States—the American Federation of Labor. The AFL was established at a labor convention held in Columbus, Ohio, in December 1886, just a little more than six months after the violence that rocked Chicago's Haymarket Square. This new organization was established on two basic principles: (1) "pure and simple unionism," which would focus exclusively on true labor issues, such as wages, hours, and working conditions, and (2) "voluntarism," a hard-line, strict reliance on the union itself and its members.[72]

From its founding, the AFL defined itself as a viable alternative to the Knights of Labor. The AFL would not spend time running candidates for public office. The new union also structured itself to keep the various affiliated unions autonomous, whereas the Knights had not. To further its claim as a choice over the Knights, the new union took up the fight for the eight-hour workday, which the Knights had failed to accomplish. AFL leaders also encouraged higher dues and membership fees to help provide an adequate war chest of funds to support long strikes. Unlike the Knights, the AFL almost exclusively encouraged membership of skilled labor, as well as white males. A look at the 13 original unions that joined the AFL reveals that only two had women members and none allowed blacks or other minorities.

The future success of the AFL might have been ensured at that founding moment when those in attendance (the Federation of Organized Trades and Labor Unions had called the convention that year) selected the new organization's first president. He was "an English immigrant of Dutch Jewish descent," who worked as a cigar maker in New York City—Samuel Gompers.[73]

SAMUEL GOMPERS

Gompers would serve as the first president of the American Federation of Labor for nearly 30 years, from 1886 until his death in 1924, with the exception of only one year. He managed to redirect the labor movement at a crucial moment in time, when the Knights of Labor were losing direction and influence and when the nation was struggling out of a severe economic depression.

In 1893, hard times hit the United States, as money issues regarding the continued reliance on silver as part of the American money supply led to a drain on the nation's gold reserves. With high tariffs creating trade problems, and farm prices tumbling because of overproduction caused by the new technologies in agriculture (such as the McCormick's harvesting machine), Americans found themselves facing factory closings, high unemployment, business and farmer bankruptcies, inflation, and a host of economic problems. The depression stretched nearly the length of President Grover Cleveland's second term, from 1893 through much of 1896.

Gompers managed to jump-start the labor movement as it emerged into the light of a new economic era of tremendous growth and expansion in the U.S. economy. A portion of that new birth of unionism of the late 1890s was led by the Cigar Makers' International Union, of which Gompers was a member. He proved to be a leader among his fellow cigar rollers and soon became a rising star in the national arena of labor organizing. Gompers was a "stocky, matter-of-fact, stubborn labor leader whose character and philosophy were in such glaring contrast to the character and philosophy of [the Knights' leader] Powderly."[74]

Samuel Gompers was born abroad, in 1850, in London's East End. He grew up watching his father, of Dutch and Jewish ancestry, make cigars, a trade young Samuel was apprenticed to learn at the age of 10. In 1863, he moved with his family to the United States, where they lived in a tenement on New York's East Side, a poor neighborhood filled with immigrants, many from central and eastern Europe. Samuel worked alongside his father making cigars until the following year, when he went out and found his own job. When he did, he immediately joined a union.

It was there in the cigar-making shops of New York's East Side that young Gompers not only worked his trade but learned new ideas about the working class, unions, and the problems facing organized labor in the United States:

> The cigar making shops at this time were schools of political and social philosophy as well as manufactories, and there was no more avid student than the young immigrant from London already steeped in the background of British trade unionism. As he sat at his bench in the dark and dusty loft, dexterously fashioning cigars, he listened with eager attention to the talk of socialism and labor reform among his fellow workers. Most of them were European-born and many of them members of the International Workingmen's Association. They had the custom of having one of their number read the labor periodicals and other magazines aloud to them (chipping in to make up the pay he would otherwise have lost) and Gompers was often given this assignment.[75]

This exposure to all the prevalent economic and socialist philosophies of his day did not turn Gompers into a political theorist, however. Instead, he formed himself into a clear-thinking, practical individual who always took a nuts-and-bolts approach to labor issues. (Gompers had even been warned by some of his cigar-making associates to be careful reading Karl Marx and Friedrich Engels and to "be constantly on guard against being carried away by their theorizing.")[76]

With his dedication to the cigar-making working class, young Gompers set out to bring new direction to the union. He had come to see the Cigar Makers' Union as a model of the future for organized labor. "From this little group came the purpose and initiative that finally resulted in the present American labor movement," he wrote later in life. "We did not create the American trade union . . . but we did create the technique and formulate the fundamentals that guided trade unions to constructive policies and achievements."[77]

Gompers was only 29 years old when he helped reorganize the Cigar Makers' International Union, and once the new direction was established, he never wavered from it. With bulldog tenacity, he stuck to his agenda for his union. For those who joined Gompers and his leadership as a union organizer, the immigrant from England was easy for them to like. Many believed "Gompers looked . . . like a labor leader."[78] He was diminutive, standing only 5 feet, 4 inches (1.63 meters) in height, with a short, barrel-shaped body. During the 1880s, his hair was black and often unkempt, and a thick walrus mustache and small patch of hair on his chin set off a strong jawline and broad face that "revealed both the force and stubbornness of his character."[79] In later years, his photographs reveal a well-dressed man with no facial hair wearing a gilt-edged set of pince-nez glasses balanced on his nose.

Depicted here in a December 1886 issue of *Harper's Weekly*, Samuel Gompers immigrated to the United States from England in 1863 and began working in the cigar-making industry. In 1886, he formed the American Federation of Labor (AFL) to represent cigar makers and other craft industries.

Gompers was always remembered as a gracious man with the qualities of a gentleman. His followers liked him for other reasons, as well, not the least of which was his accessibility. Gompers never removed himself from the average worker, even when he became an important and influential labor organizer. Gompers had a reputation for his friendliness and easygoing nature. He enjoyed a night out on the town, and he counted among his favorite social endeavors "beer parlors, the theater, music halls, show girls, and the Atlantic City boardwalk."[80] When the moment called for serious business, Gompers was always ready to play his part. During social gatherings, however, he put his business character aside, chomped on a big cigar, and enjoyed a stein of beer. His rivals at the Knights of Labor took advantage of his penchant for a drink by publishing a pamphlet noting the rarity of having "the pleasure of seeing Mr. Gompers sober."[81] Despite such tendencies, Gompers was an easy man for many in the Cigar Makers' Union to follow.

The organization of the AFL in 1886 actually had its roots in earlier events, dating from 1881. That year, labor leaders from throughout the country met in Pittsburgh. This meeting included delegates from many different trade unions, as well as the Knights of Labor. The purpose of the conference was to establish an umbrella association that as many unions as possible would feel compelled to join. Rivalry between labor groups was seen as a negative, an element that sometimes stalled the advance of the working class. Gompers, representing the Cigar Makers' Union, was present at that 1881 meeting and was chosen to chair the organizing committee. (At the time, he was still a member of the Knights of Labor, having joined back in the 1870s.)

During sessions, Gompers fought to make any new organization "a strictly trade union affair."[82] Seemingly, at every turn, Gompers was defeated in this effort, but a new organization was established—the Federation of Organized Trades and Labor Unions (FOTLU). Its purpose was to create solidarity within the labor movement and to focus on the establishment of an eight-hour workday, the abolition of child labor, and the repeal of "conspiracy" laws, which still defined some union activity as nothing more than conspiratorial.

The Federation, however, was doomed even as it was created. The Knights of Labor did not give its support, and many other national unions also jumped ship. Only a handful of delegates attended the Federation's annual meeting the following year, and Gompers, who was elected the organization's president in 1883, did not even attend that year's meeting. By 1886, the Federation was on its last leg. That year, during the meeting in December, held in Columbus, Ohio, those present represented 25 labor groups, including the Cigar Makers. After much discussion, the American Federation of Labor (AFL) was formed, and Gompers was chosen as its first president.

RUNNING THE AFL

So much of what the AFL became immediately after its founding and in the years that followed centered around its leader, Samuel Gompers. He surrounded himself with a skilled group of loyal followers, and "it was he who gave the new organization life and direction."[83] Gompers was generally cautious about thinking of himself as too important. Of his leadership of the AFL, he would later write: "There was much work, little pay, and very little honor."[84] He established his office without ego, first using a room no larger than 8 feet by 10 feet (about 2.5 meters by 3 meters). There were few pieces of furniture "other than a kitchen table, some crates for chairs, and a filing case made out of tomato boxes."[85]

Gompers, however, was a wholly driven man, who exuded excitement and worked tirelessly. He was constantly writing letters (which were not typed, but written in his own hand) to labor leaders across the United States. He edited a publication, the *Trade Union Advocate*, to put the word out to new unions whose members might be interested in joining the AFL. His office collected union dues, issued charters to new member unions, and handled a constant movement of paperwork. Even then, he continuously attended meetings and national conventions and traveled on speaking tours. Slowly but efficiently, Samuel Gompers "transformed the American Federation of Labor from a purely paper organization into a militant and powerful champion of labor's rights."[86] For nearly 40 years, Gompers continued a labor campaign he likened to a crusade, "a holy cause."[87]

His efforts would not fail. During the AFL's early years, its rivalry with the Knights of Labor was ongoing. When some efforts were made to unite the AFL and the Knights into a single organization, Gompers opposed the move. "Talk of harmony with the Knights of Labor is bosh," he said. "They are just as great enemies of trade unions as any employer can be, only more vindictive. It is no use trying to placate them or even to be friendly."[88] Unity between larger labor organizations would never become a goal of the uncompromising Samuel Gompers.

With each passing year, the Knights faded further into irrelevance and the AFL grew into a vibrant organization. Growth was slow, however. The AFL's original member unions numbered 150,000 workers in 1886. Even by 1892, the membership of the AFL was only 250,000. These were, of course, difficult years for organized labor, with many industrialists and large business owners trying to oppress unions in the courts and through government legislation. The Panic of 1893 only made matters worse. Gompers was not distracted, though, and chose to keep his course and his goals for the AFL on target.

It should be noted, however, that despite Gompers's dogged campaign to establish the AFL as a major cornerstone of the labor movement of the late 1880s and early 1890s, the fact remains that the AFL was only important to a point. During these key years when the union movement was taking new direction, the real basis for the new unionism was the national unions themselves, not the AFL. As one historian states: "[The national unions] could exist without the A.F. of L., but the A.F. of L. had no meaning without them."[89] The national unions were autonomous, and they controlled the local unions that made up their membership.

In addition, the AFL's structure and ideals always worked against broadening its membership. The AFL did not allow Asians as members, and Gompers himself fought hard in 1892 and 1902 for the continuation of the Chinese Exclusion Act, which banned Chinese workers from immigrating to the United States. After the turn of the century, AFL leaders supported limitations on the number of immigrants entering the United States from eastern and southern Europe, including Poles, Greeks, Italians, Hungarians, and others. The AFL Executive Council, the organization's leadership body, allowed only those national unions that exclusively admitted white workers. Beginning in 1891, the AFL did allow black men to take on roles as strike organizers, but, even as late as 1900, the organization continued to support the idea of segregated local unions.

There were other strategies that did not help the AFL gain membership and may well have held the organization back in its advance as a leading institution among labor organizations:

> From day one, moreover, the AFL's basic organizing strategy undercut its capacity to promote labor solidarity irrespective of color, nationality, and sex. The stress on craft unionism, together with hefty dues and initiation fees, inevitably distanced the Federation from workers outside the skilled, relatively high-paying trades. A great many of those outsiders were native-born white men; but women, immigrants, and workers of color were all

disproportionately confined to unskilled and semiskilled occupations, where craft unionism—not to mention expensive unionism—simply did not make sense.[90]

There were additional weaknesses that caused problems for the AFL, not the least of which were assaults on the organization and its members during the 1890s by wealthy capitalists who ran the nation's largest railroads, mining operations, and factory systems. One of the strongest such attacks on the AFL took place during the summer and fall of 1892 when an AFL union, the Amalgamated Association of Iron and Steel Workers, fought one of the wealthiest men in the country, a Scottish steel baron named Andrew Carnegie.

FACING OFF WITH CARNEGIE

During the summer of 1892, the Amalgamated, working in a mill in Homestead, Pennsylvania, was faced with being pushed out of existence. The steel- and ironworkers were skilled but represented only 1 of every 4 of the nearly 4,000 workers in the steel mill, and they were the best paid. Their contract was set to expire on June 30—that summer—and the steel plant's owner, Andrew Carnegie, was prepared to stand against the unionized steelworkers, wanting no one who worked for him in the Homestead plant to be a member of a union. With that goal in his sights, Carnegie turned the responsibility of making it happen to his mill manager, Henry Clay Frick. Frick already had a reputation throughout western Pennsylvania as a no-nonsense manager who despised labor unions and would do anything to destroy them and otherwise crush their capacity to go out on strike.

Before the steelworkers' contract expired, Frick began playing his hand. He made it clear in late spring there would be no new union contract by announcing that the union member' wages would be cut on July 1 by an

In 1889, Henry Clay Frick was appointed chairman of Carnegie Brothers and Company to help reorganize that organization. Although he successfully made Carnegie the largest steel manufacturer in the world, he drew the ire of union laborers for attempting to force them out of the company.

average of 22 percent. On May 30, a month before the end of the steelworkers' contract, Frick made a second announcement: If the steelworkers did not accept the reduction in their wages within a week of the expiration of their union contract, the Carnegie mill would no longer recognize the workers' union. The workers stood their ground, however, and refused to accept the concessions Frick tried to force on them. Frick responded by hiring private, Pinkerton detectives and closing down the mill on June 30. He then allowed the Pinkertons to provide security as they hired new, nonunion, "scab" workers to replace the ousted steelworkers.

Unfortunately for Frick, his moves against the steelworkers angered not only the Carnegie steelworkers, but nearly every one of the 11,000 workers and residents in Homestead, Pennsylvania. When the steelworkers struck and set up pickets outside the plant's gates, they were joined by unskilled steelworkers, mostly eastern European immigrants, together with their wives and children. Other skilled steel- and ironworkers at other Carnegie plants also struck at their mills in support of the Amalgamated at the Homestead.

After a week of the strike, the Pinkerton force took drastic measures. In the early morning hours of July 6, about 300 well-armed Pinkerton agents were floated down the Monongahela River on barges and landed on the river's banks close to the steel plant, hoping they could sneak to the plant and take control of the facility and grounds before the strikers saw them. Things did not go well. They were spotted by strikers, and a clash soon ensued. Along the banks of the Monongahela, detectives and strikers exchanged gunfire. The violent clash stretched on through most of the day, leaving seven workers and three Pinkerton agents dead.

Spurred by this bloody violence, Pennsylvania governor Robert Pattison sent 8,000 state militia troops to secure the Homestead plant, which they managed to accomplish on July 12. For the union workers, the troops represented their rescue. One of the union leaders addressed the newly arrived troops thus: "On behalf of the Amalgamated Association I wish to say that after suffering an attack of illegal authority, we are glad to have the legal authority of the state here."[91]

It soon became clear, however, that the soldiers were not present to aid the workers. In fact, they had been called at the request of Henry Frick. The militia was there only to take control of the factory. Before the month of August, the mill was employing scab labor, recruited by the Pinkertons, and was protected by the Pennsylvania State Militia.

This success was not enough for Frick. He, after all, was under orders from Carnegie to force the union out once and for all. He appealed to local judges to issue indictments against the union leaders who had organized the strike on charges of murder, conspiracy, and treason. (As to the treason charge, the workers had technically engaged in the "usurpation of the civil authority.")[92] Frick's call for the indictments was aided by an event that occurred on July 2, when a New York anarchist, Alexander Berkman, attempted to kill the steel plant manager. The situation was getting out of hand, and the city's police chief decided to take drastic measures and arrest the union workers. During the following months, the courts issued 185 indictments, with some union leaders being indicted four or five times each. Although no convictions were made against the union workers, the legal fees to defend them nearly bankrupted the union's strike fund.

By November, the strike against the Homestead Mill was still ongoing, but support was waning. The unskilled workers wanted out of their agreement to support the strike. The Amalgamated workers, disappointed and feeling defeated, decided to end their strike, accepting failure. There were other losers, including the steel- and ironworkers at other Carnegie plants who had supported their colleagues. The Amalgamated lost membership from those plants, as well. The upshot was clear and a bitter pill for organized labor: The Amalgamated lost two-thirds of its membership (24,000 dropped to 8,000). Carnegie was the big winner, for

HARPER'S WEEKLY

JOURNAL OF CIVILIZATION

Vol. XXXVI.—No. 1854.
Copyright, 1892, by Harper & Brothers.
All Rights Reserved.

NEW YORK, SATURDAY, JULY 16, 1892.

TEN CENTS A COPY.
FOUR DOLLARS A YEAR.

THE HOMESTEAD RIOT.—Drawn by W. P. Snyder after a Photograph by Dabbs, Pittsburg.—[See Page 678.]
THE PINKERTON MEN LEAVING THE BARGES AFTER THE SURRENDER.

On June 30, 1882, the Amalgamated Association of Iron and Steel Workers, which represented the skilled iron- and steelworkers at Carnegie Steel Company, went on strike in support of better wages and working conditions. Known as the Homestead Strike, the confrontation lasted until November 20, when the workers agreed to return to the job as nonunion laborers.

his mills had thrown off a powerful union and those plants remained nonunion for the next 40 years. (In a few years, Carnegie would sell off his steel empire to another tycoon, Wall Street financier J. Pierpont Morgan, and Morgan's new conglomerate was renamed United States Steel.)

THE PULLMAN STRIKE

The events of 1892 that had swirled around the Homestead steel mill in Pennsylvania did great damage to the union movement, as well as to the AFL. Two years later, however, another labor disaster hit the unions, this time in Illinois. The labor conflict there sprang from events that stretched back to the early 1890s. Prior to that time, American railroad workers had received little support from the craft union movement of the previous decade. Railroad workers had not chosen to join the AFL but instead had remained members of the five organizations known as the Railroad Brotherhoods, one each for engineers, conductors, firefighters, brake operators, and switch operators. Each group organized independently, not only of other unions, but even of one another. Their membership constituted skilled, semiskilled, and unskilled labor. (They did not allow blacks as members.) The five Brotherhoods generally did not like to strike, although their members remained relatively low paid for industrial laborers, averaging only $350 in annual wages. In time, the railroad workers grew tired of accepting such concessions; in addition, they often worked under dangerous conditions and each year, on average, lost one of every 100 of their number to a railroad accident.

By the fall of 1892, when the Amalgamated steelworkers were struggling through their strike against Carnegie, railroad workers met secretly in Chicago to form a new labor organization—the American Railway Union (ARU). This new organization announced its existence publicly on June 20, 1893, and its leaders threw their arms open to all white railroad workers (except executive officials and superintendents). The new organization's first president was Eugene Victor Debs. The son of French immigrants, Debs, a thin, balding man, was a socialist who opposed the "oppressions" of capitalism. He began working as a railroad firefighter at age 15. More recently, he had served in the Indiana state legislature. Within a year of Debs's taking the presidency of the American Railroad Union, the labor organization's membership rocketed to 150,000.

Debs wasted little time organizing his new union before calling for a strike against the Great Northern Railroad in the spring of 1894. The strike, lasting only 18 days, brought an agreement from the railroad's president, James Hill, to raise wages. (Prior to the strike, the railroad workers on the Great Northern were among the lowest paid in the country.) Already growing in numbers, the successful strike resulted in an increase in the membership of the ARU at the rate of 2,000 a day.

Emboldened by his success, Debs next targeted the Pullman Palace Car Company plant in Pullman, Illinois, outside Chicago. George Pullman had been in the business of producing various types of railroad cars—including sleeping cars, dining cars, parlor cars, and private cars—for nearly 30 years. In the 1860s, he had opened his factory near Chicago and built an entire town (named after him), where he housed his employees, who in turn paid him high rents even as he paid them low wages. He represented just the kind of capitalist that Debs despised. He described the company's founder in less than glowing terms:

> I believe a rich plunderer like Pullman is a greater felon
> than a poor thief, and it has become no small part of the
> duty of this organization to strip the mask of hypocrisy
> from the pretended philanthropist and show him to the

world as an oppressor of labor. . . . The paternalism of Pullman is the same as the interest of a slave holder in his human chattels.[93]

When Debs ordered the strike against the Pullman Company, just a month after his successful strike against the Great Northern, Pullman responded immediately by closing his factory. The next month, striking workers attended the ARU's first national convention and called for support from their fellow workers: "It is victory or death . . . to you we confide our cause . . . do not desert us as you hope not to be deserted."[94] Union convention delegates agreed, calling for a boycott by all ARU workers on June 26. By that date, no ARU members would handle any train that included any Pullman cars.

The ARU boycott expanded into a general railroad strike. Even though the Railroad Brotherhoods objected, the strike soon involved 150,000 sympathetic railroad workers. The wheels of 11 American railroads—including the Illinois Central; the Chicago & Northwestern; and the Atchison, Topeka & Santa Fe—screeched to a halt.

Within the first 48 hours of the strike, and with the nation's rail system at a virtual standstill, larger elements came into play. Government officials, including President Grover Cleveland, U.S. Attorney General Richard Olney, Army General John Schofield, and Secretary of War Daniel Lamont, kept tabs on the strike from Washington, D.C. The railroad stoppage was halting the delivery of the U.S. mail. Attorney General Olney advised the president to demand that the strikers put a halt to their actions, even though Debs claimed the strike was not about stopping mail delivery; it was just about demanding that the railroads not use Pullman cars.

Nevertheless, Olney, with advice from the railroads' General Managers' Association, decided to get a court

Eugene V. Debs, who later founded the Socialist Party of America, became president of the American Railway Union in 1893. Debs led a successful strike against the Great Northern Railroad to restore workers' wages, but his bid to challenge the Pullman Palace Car Company failed. Debs is depicted in this *Harper's Weekly* cartoon as king of the railroads after his victory over the Great Northern.

injunction against the ARU based on an 1890 law, the Sherman Antitrust Act, "a vaguely worded and rarely invoked federal law directed against monopolies involved in interstate trade."[95] On July 2, Olney claimed the ARU was engaging in actions that interfered with interstate commerce and constituted conspiracy to halt the delivery of the U.S. mail. According to Olney, the ARU and the Pullman strikers had created an illegal trust, which the government had the right to break up, because the strikers' actions constituted a violation of federal law. The attorney general presented the injunction to Eugene V. Debs in person, and soon it appeared in newspapers throughout the country. Although most newspapers sided with Olney's claims, the *New York Times* referred to the injunction as a "Gatling gun on paper" and "a veritable dragnet in matter of legal verbiage."[96]

The injunction was issued on July 2, and, the following day, President Cleveland called up federal troops to enforce it. Neither the president nor his attorney general informed Governor Altgeld they were sending soldiers to Chicago. When he received word, he was furious, because the U.S. Constitution places the power of ordering troops into a specific state in the hands of the governor or the state legislature. The troops were there, though, arriving in Chicago on the Fourth of July.

Almost immediately, riots broke out between the soldiers and the strikers. The rail yards of the Illinois Central (IC) were the site of bloody encounters, and fires nearly destroyed the IC rail yards. Elsewhere across the city, fires broke out, some set by "the hoodlum element in the city."[97] Some fires were set at Chicago's Columbian Exposition, the massive World's Fair, and several buildings were destroyed in Jackson Park. There probably was no connection between these fires and the strikers, but the public blamed them, anyway. Less than a week later, Eugene V. Debs, president of the ARU, and other union officials were under arrest.

The ARU officials might not have understood by that time, but the strike they had helped organize was a failure. An emergency ARU committee called for a general strike across Chicago to give support to the Pullman workers, but that call only produced 25,000 sympathetic laborers on July 5. Most unions held off until they heard what the AFL leader, Samuel Gompers, was going to do. Gompers arrived in Chicago on

(continues on page 104)

INVESTIGATING THE AFTERMATH OF PULLMAN

The Great Pullman Railroad Strike of 1894 had caused great unrest within the labor movement. Many thought the strike had gotten out of control, because the conflict between the railroad workers and railroad management had escalated to include the court system, the governor of Illinois, the president of the United States, the Illinois state militia, and even federal troops. In the aftermath of the labor conflict, President Cleveland thought it important to determine exactly what had happened and its cost. Six years earlier, the U.S. Congress had passed a law called the Arbitration Act. This act authorized Congress to provide federal mediators to help settle labor disputes when requested by unions and their employers. The act also established special commissions to examine labor disputes and determine what had taken place. It was this law that Cleveland evoked following the Pullman Strike.

Just two weeks after the strike, President Cleveland appointed a three-person commission, including Carroll Wright, the U.S. commissioner of labor, to look into the strike, why it had happened, and what was its results. He gave instructions to the commissioners to "hear all persons interested therein who may come before it."* The other two members were Nicholas Worthington, a lawyer and former Illinois congressman, and New Yorker John Kernan.

The hearings were held in a Chicago post office, beginning on August 15 and lasting two weeks. The commission also held a one-day hearing in Washington, D.C., where they invited anyone who wanted to testify to do so. In all, the commissioners heard testimony from 109 witnesses. Once they concluded their hearings, the three men wrote a 54-page analysis titled *Report on the Chicago Strike of June–July, 1894*. Attached to the report were nearly 700 pages of sworn testimony, which began to tell the story behind the strike and its results. Because of the strike, the railroads affected sustained nearly $700,000 in property damage and $4 million in lost business. The Pullman strikers lost $350,000 in lost wages, and their supporting railroad workers lost four times that amount.

Other statistics in the report refer to more sobering and even disturbing details. A dozen people had been shot and killed during the strike. Law enforcement officials had arrested more than 500 people. Those who fought the strikers included more than 1,900 federal troops, 4,000 Illinois militiamen, 5,000 deputy marshals, and 3,000 Chicago police officers.

The report also included an analysis of other aspects of the strike, most of which did not relate to numbers but more to the impact the strike had even as it was going on. The commissioners noted the strong resolve of the strikers; the attempt by the railroads to destroy the strike and its supporters; the opportunity it gave for outsiders to participate in looting, burning, and even murder; and the suffering experienced by the families of the strikers. One aspect of the report that was highly critical of the railroads was their reliance on the General Managers' Association, which was in fact illegal. The commissioners referred to this railroad group as "an illustration of the persistent and shrewdly devised plans of corporations to overreach . . . and usurp powers and rights."**

Throughout their report, the three commissioners found plenty of blame to go around. They noted that strikers had broken their contracts with the railroads, while also recognizing that the Pullman Company and the General Managers' Association had failed to accept arbitration proposals or even peaceful settlement of the labor dispute. They also pointed out that the Managers' Association had armed and paid for 3,600 guards who were deputized by U.S. marshals. By doing so, "these men were taking orders from the railroad but exercising the power of the United States."***

The commissioners ended their report with several assessments and suggestions, which included calling for (1) the establishment of a permanent U.S. Strike Commission, (2) greater use of arbitration on the part of the states where strikes might take place, and (3) the recognition of labor unions by employers. So thoroughly did the

(continues)

(continued)

commissioners complete their task of analyzing the Pullman Strike and the resulting American Railroad Strike that few were able to criticize their work.

   * Rosemary Laughlin, *The Pullman Strike of 1894: American Labor Comes of Age* (Greensboro, N.C.: Morgan Reynolds, 2000), 73.
  ** Ibid., 76.
 *** Ibid., 80.

(continued from page 101)

July 12 and met with other AFL officials at the city's Briggs House Hotel. The AFL leaders decided to call for Debs to end the boycott in exchange for ARU workers to return to their jobs as if nothing had happened. Almost immediately, the strike called by Debs was over. In the intervening months, Debs and others were tried and several convicted, including the ARU president who served six months in jail. The failed Pullman Strike struck the death knell for the ARU. By 1897, the powerful railroad labor organization was defunct.

LEARNING FROM LOSS

The labor movement in general and its leadership specifically emerged from the dual defeats of the Homestead strike and the Pullman disaster having learned different lessons. ARU President Debs and his socialist associates felt it was time for all unions to band together, to unite the working class of America into a mass of solidarity. Samuel Gompers was less convinced. He chose to stick to his original plan and strategy of union organizing—"pure and simple unionism."[98] Gompers and other craft union leaders decided it was impossible to stand against the linked powers of corporate business and government authorities who cooperated with them against unions. Gompers wanted labor to further win over converts among politicians and business leaders already sympathetic to their cause. The vote might be the key, Gompers thought: "The ballots of workingmen from the [old] parties would bring a higher plane of prosperity."[99] Neither Republicans nor Democrats had adequately supported the labor movement at any time during the nineteenth century. With a new century approaching, some labor leaders had hopes for another political movement, one with reform in mind, including social and economic changes friendly to the working class—the progressive movement.

7

Labor and the New Century

Party politics and the labor movement had rarely found common ground throughout the nineteenth century. The two main parties—Democrats and Republicans—not only had failed to embrace the labor movement, but also had generally been antagonistic toward it. During the 1890s, a third political party, the Populists, emerged, supported by American farmers, as well as wage earners, factory workers, and some unions. When formed in Omaha, Nebraska, in the summer of 1892, the Populists did call for a shorter workday, quotas on immigration, and government ownership of all railroads and telephone and telegraph companies. What members the Knights of Labor were left with in the 1890s (fewer than 75,000) generally gave their support to the Populists.

The Populists' prolabor agenda was a short list, however, and such leaders as Samuel Gompers never warmed up to the new party, in part because it courted employers as much as it did employees. Although Gompers did not fully approve of the Populists, the AFL did give some support to the party, even if the Federation's national convention in 1894 rejected the Populist socialist call for government ownership of much of America's means of production. Ultimately, the Populist Party failed to become a powerful enough party to control any element of American politics. (The party's last candidate for president, William Jennings Bryan from Nebraska, came within 500,000 votes of defeating the Republican candidate, William McKinley, in 1896, but only because the Democrats had chosen Bryan as their candidate.) After the 1896 election, the party began slipping out of existence.

The new political hope for the labor movement emerged even before the arrival of the new century. By the 1890s, a large framed social movement began to take shape, first led by "old-fashioned evangelists and moral reformers [who] campaigned to eradicate drinking, gambling, and prostitution."[100] The movement quickly spread to include many middle-class reformers who had additional ideas about the need for reform in the United States. These "Progressives" hoped to elevate the underclass of people in the United States, eliminate poverty, and give opportunities to the poor. They sought political reforms, including the secret ballot, the direct election of senators, and the institutionalization of the initiative, the referendum, and the recall. They wanted to clean up American politics, expose corruption, and push government to take a more active role in protecting its people through new laws covering everything from housing safety codes to bans on child labor to health standards in factories that produce food.

It was an ambitious movement, one that stretched from the 1890s until the years following World War I and even beyond. Unlike the socialist call of such men as Eugene Debs, who sought to completely redefine the basic institutions of power in the United States, the Progressives chose to work within the existing institutions to bring about change. They were not interested in tearing down the house; they just wanted to make it better, safer, stronger, fairer, more equitable, and even more democratic.

Some of the Progressives' agenda directly impacted the working men and women of the country. States began to pass laws that restricted the abuse of children in the work-

(continues on page 110)

THE CAMPAIGN AGAINST CHILD LABOR

As America's workforce became organized through labor unions and trades organizations, these groups set agendas for themselves that typically called for higher wages, better working conditions, and even the right to organize as a union. Often, an additional goal was also included on the list of many unions and labor groups: restrictions on the use of child labor. During the nineteenth and early twentieth centuries, American children were employed in every conceivable industry, from glassworks to mining, fish canneries to field labor. There were so many children working that labor unions considered them rivals for jobs that would otherwise be taken by adults. The National Labor Union, the Knights of Labor, the Federation of Organized Trades and Labor Unions, and the American Federation of Labor all supported drastic restrictions on child labor.

Although child labor could not be considered the backbone of the American workforce, there were many young workers. The U.S. Census of 1880 revealed a startling statistic: more than one million wage workers in the country were under the age of 16. Child labor could be found everywhere in America during the latter decades of the nineteenth century, but some parts of the country relied more heavily on young workers than did other regions. Across the South, child workers were employed to save costs in industrial workplaces from iron and steel plants to cotton textile mills. In 1896, one out of every four textile workers in North Carolina was under the age of 16, while only 5 percent of such workers in Massachusetts were children.

Child labor was always commonplace in the United States because younger workers could be employed cheaper than adults and were too young to complain when they were forced to accept jobs offering poor conditions and almost no benefits. In fact, one of the major criticisms of child labor given by its critics was that such workers gained little from the work arrangement. Not all work done by children could be considered exploitative, however. Few in America had problems with children working the occasional odd job after school or with parents who expected their children to do work around the house or farm—which benefited the whole family.

There were few people who did not support the traditional system of having younger workers work for an adult as an apprentice or trainee to learn a skill or a trade in exchange for room and board. Those who fought against child labor did not target the family farm or the apprentice system. "There is work that profits children," said Lewis Hine, a turn-of-the-century photographer who led a crusade against child labor during which he photographed young workers to document child labor abuses, "and there is work that brings profit only to employers. The object of employing children is not to train them, but to get high profits from their work."*

Some people did choose to defend child labor by arguing that the work required of children was not particularly grueling or difficult. Such supporters did not truly understand the nature of many of the jobs done by child workers. The hours were often as long as those for adults and the work conditions just as substandard as with older laborers. The work they did was often monotonous, physically demanding, and detrimental to their health.

Laws were passed against child labor, but they were few and far between. In 1893, Illinois became one of the first states to pass labor laws to protect children (as well as women). By the early twentieth century, the campaign to bring an end to abusive child labor hit its stride. Several states passed laws that capped the number of hours a child could be employed in a week and established a minimum wage for young workers. These early laws were often written in ways that made it easy for employers to dodge their intent, however. In addition, most states that passed such laws did little to enforce them.

One of the key organizations that supported restrictions for child labor was the National Child Labor Committee, which was formed in 1904. Those who joined the group "believed that a healthy, happy, normal childhood was the rightful heritage of all children." The group set standards for child labor that were intended to benefit young workers; these called for the eight-hour workday, the elimination of all night work for children, and work permits that clearly included the age of the child in question and required proof of that

(continues)

(continued)

age. Also, the organization encouraged the enforcement of compulsory school-attendance laws. Despite their well-intended goals, legislation came slowly and haphazardly. Child labor would continue to be a social and labor issue well into the twentieth century. Child labor only began to drop dramatically in numbers during the Great Depression of the 1930s. With so many adults losing their jobs because of the poor economy, the market for child labor declined as adults agreed to work many of the jobs that young people had been employed at during better economic times.

Strong federal legislation limiting child labor did not come about until 1938. That year, President Franklin Roosevelt signed a congressional bill creating the Fair Labor Standards Act, which, among other things, put significant restrictions on the employment of children. Under the act, children under the age of 16 could not be used in factory, manufacturing, or mining jobs. By 1949, Congress amended its original legislation to include other businesses, including agriculture, transportation, communications, and public utilities. Even jobs not closed off to younger workers were open to children under 16 only during after-school hours and on weekends.

---

* Russell Freedman, *Kids at Work: Lewis Hine and the Crusade Against Child Labor* (New York: Clarion Books, 1994), 21.

(continued from page 107)

place, limited the work hours of women and young people, set new safety standards for work environments, and created funds to compensate workers injured on their jobs.

During these years of Progressive reform, the labor movement was largely embodied in the efforts of three competing labor organizations. The American Federation of Labor had survived the 1893 depression (the first American labor federation to do so) and was still under the leadership of Samuel Gompers. Craft unionism, "pure and simple," was still Gompers's mantra. The two other labor-related groups of significance were much more radicalized: the Socialist Party of America (SP) and the Industrial Workers of the World (IWW), popularly known as "the Wobblies."

All three groups felt they were competing for the attention of the American worker, and each offered "a different program for winning better working conditions, richer lives, and social justice." The AFL was placing much of its emphasis on collective bargaining, which featured "contracts negotiated by professional representatives for well-funded unions of highly skilled workers, organized according to their separate crafts."[101] Gompers was also going after the unorganized workers by creating a system of "federal labor unions" (FLUs) to provide membership for laborers who were not craft workers, the original backbone of the AFL. Gompers had decided that the craft union approach was too narrow. The AFL was going out of its way to bring into its fold women, immigrants, and minority workers, such as blacks and Hispanics, even as the labor organization continued to reject Asian workers. The change in tack paid off: By 1904, the AFL boasted 1.67 million members in 120 union groups, an increase of more than 1.4 million and a doubling of the number of member unions compared to 1897. Despite some later setbacks (the organization actually declined in membership in 1905), growth for the AFL continued through World War I, with a total of 3 million members by 1917.

Opposition to unions during this period appeared just as strong as ever, and violent acts were perpetuated by and against union workers. In 1910, 20 workers at an AFL printing shop in Los Angeles were killed by a bomb. Ironworkers blew up 87 steel bridges and other structures built with nonunion workers, resulting in the indictments of two union members for murder. Such acts caused Republican President William Howard Taft, during his reelection campaign in 1912, to

During the 1912 presidential campaign, Democratic candidate Woodrow Wilson announced his support for labor unions and subsequently received the endorsement of the AFL. Wilson further reduced the power of trusts and showed his support for labor by pushing the Clayton Antitrust Act through Congress.

speak out against the unions, for "lawlessness in labor disputes."[102] On the other hand, Taft's Democratic challenger, the progressive governor of New Jersey, Woodrow Wilson, gave his endorsement in support of the workers' right to organize into unions and won the election with the return endorsement of the AFL.

During Wilson's first year in office, the labor movement experienced one of its saddest setbacks. Justice Department officials issued indictments against the leaders of the AFL-affiliated United Mine Workers on conspiracy charges, because of their efforts to organize all miners into a labor organization. Meanwhile, in southern Colorado, members of the United Mine Workers launched a strike against Colorado Fuel & Iron (CF&I), owned by John D. Rockefeller Jr.

On September 23, 1913, as many as 11,000 striking miners and their families set up tent colonies, where they lived during the strike, many having been forced out of their CF&I camps by mine guards on the opening day of the strike. That day, a harsh blizzard swept through the region of the strike and "for fifty miles around, out of the mouths of the canyons straggled the 9,000 striking miners with their women and children."[103] The strike dragged on for months, even as company officials, with support from the Colorado militia, used scab labor in the mines. During those months, scattered violence occurred between the strikers and those hired by the mining company to break the strike. Agents of the Baldwin-Felts Detective Agency were called in, and they occasionally raided the striking miners' encampments. On one occasion, near Trinidad, Colorado,

> an armored automobile, made in the shops of the Colorado Fuel & Iron Company . . . was armed with a Hotchkiss machine gun capable of shooting 400 times a minute, and with a ball that would kill a man at a range of more than a mile. Manned with five deputies, three of them at least being Baldwin-Felts gunmen, this automobile made the trip to [one of the mining camps][104]

where the machine gun was used to blast the strikers' camp apart: "One hundred and forty-seven bullets were put through one tent; a boy 15 years old was shot nine times in the legs; one miner was killed, shot through the forehead.

This was but one of a series of incidents."[105] Angry armed miners naturally fought back during and after such attacks. Then, with emotions running high, disaster struck on April 20, 1914, when militia troops advanced on the mining tent colony based at Ludlow. The famous socialist author John Reed would write about the attack against the miners:

> Suddenly, without warning . . . machine guns pounded stab-stab-stab full on the tents. It was premeditated and merciless. Militiamen have told me that their orders were to destroy the tent colony and everything living in it. . . . Suddenly the terrible storm of lead from the machine guns ripped their coverings to pieces, and the most awful panic followed. Some of the women and children streamed out over the plain, to get away from the tent colony. They were shot at as they ran.[106]

Militia troops arrived on the scene, more than 100 soldiers of Troop A. Although they arrived later in the day, they delivered two more machine guns to the attack. One officer, Lieutenant Karl Linderfelt, ordered his men to "shoot every God damned thing that moves!"[107] The attack went on most of the day and into the evening. Near sundown, militia converged on the abandoned strikers' colony and began to burn the miners' tents with kerosene and "in the flickering light of the burning tents the militia shot at the refugees again and again."[108]

The event that unfolded in the barren mountain country around Trinidad, Colorado, would become known as the Ludlow Massacre. The death toll included 21 victims shot or burned, including 11 children. An eyewitness grimly described the massacre's aftermath:

> The tent colony, or where the tent colony had been, was a great square of ghastly ruins. Stoves, pots and pans still full of food that had been cooking that terrible morning, baby carriages, piles of half-burned clothes, children's

toys all riddled with bullets, the scorched mouths of the tent cellars, and the children's toys that we found at the bottom of the "death hole"—this was all that remained of the entire worldly possessions of 1,200 poor people.[109]

The attacks did not stop after only a day, but continued on into the following month, when federal troops were called in to stop the violence. By then, a total of 66 miners or members of their families had been killed. Stubbornly, the miners continued their strike for another seven months. By year's end, they finally accepted their defeat and returned to their jobs.

The Ludlow Massacre did have a positive effect on the labor movement, however. The U.S. Congress passed and President Wilson signed the Clayton Act in October 1914, which affirmed that labor unions or organizations must not be "construed to be illegal combinations in restraint of trade under the antitrust laws." The new law also forbade the use of injunctions by the courts against "peaceful and lawful" strikes.[110] The organized labor movement applauded the act. Gompers himself saw the act as "an industrial Magna Carta."[111]

THE SOCIALIST PARTY

A second labor organization of the early twentieth century, a rival to the AFL, was the Socialist Party of America, established in 1901. Its organizers were a coalition of former Knights of Labor members, refugees from the failed Populist Party, and workers from a variety of socialist groups of which Germans and Russian Jews comprised the membership base. It was the intent of the SP to utilize their members' votes to influence the role of government toward labor. In short, the Socialist Party sought government ownership of the means of production, including factories, mills, mines, and railroads. Its new leader was the former head of the

American Railway Union—Eugene V. Debs. During the early twentieth century, the SP ran Debs several times as their presidential candidate. (In the 1912 election, Debs ran from his jail cell.) The organization found supporters among those who had given up on the two main political parties for the answers to the problems of the working class. By 1910, the SP operated 3,000 local organizations. Within two years, the Socialists had managed to elect 2,000 of their members to political offices. One was a U.S. congressman, elected from New York City's Lower East Side. It was during the hard winter of 1909–1910 that the Socialist Party organized a widespread strike in New York that featured women who worked in the garment industry as sweatshop labor. So many members of the Ladies Garment Workers (LGW) union joined the work stoppage that the strike was called the "Rising of the 20,000."

THE WOBBLIES

The third labor organization of the early 1900s was the Industrial Workers of the World—the Wobblies. The organization was formed during a June 1905 meeting of about 200 unions held in Chicago. The convention was called by the Western Federation of Miners (WFM), a nonaligned union made up of metal miners, led by the flamboyant and outspoken William "Big Bill" Haywood. The new organization was radical in nature from the beginning. Its original constitution included the hard-line conviction: "The working class and the employing class have nothing in common."[112]

The radical Wobblies believed that the labor movement in the United States would only succeed when the masses of the working class were excluded from voting and from their affiliations with the AFL. The approach and strategy of the IWW—called syndicalism—was clear from day one.

The Industrial Workers of the World, or "Wobblies," was established in 1905. Largely composed of anarchists, socialists, and radical trade unionists from throughout the United States, the union opposed the policies of the American Federation of Labor. Here, a group of Wobblies demonstrates in New York City in April 1914.

It included "taking 'direction action' on the job to build industrial unions until they were strong enough to launch a general strike and take over business and government."[113] The Wobblies expected to outlast all other labor organizations until they had literally organized workers around the world into, as they used the term: "One Big Union," the IWW. Then, as one of their members imagined, "the workers of the world . . . [would] have nothing to do but fold their arms and the world will stop."[114]

Growth and acceptance of the IWW proved slow. In 1909, the organization gained national attention and a boost in membership after its members won a strike against a Pennsylvania company that existed within the conglomerate,

U.S. Steel. Then, three years later, the Wobblies won another work stoppage—known as the "Bread and Roses Strike"—which featured 25,000 textile workers representing a dozen ethnic groups, in Lawrence, Massachusetts. Having thwarted efforts by the textile industrialists to smash the strike, the strikers pulled off a victory after two months of confrontation and occasional violence. Even with these successes, by 1915, after a decade as an organization, the IWW only included about 15,000 members. After World War I, the Wobblies organization might have included as many as 100,000 members, as many joined after a particularly bloody strike among IWW iron miners in Minnesota's Mesabi Range. Even at their height of influence, however, the Socialist Party and the IWW had a combined membership that was less than 10 percent of the membership of the AFL.

A NEW CONSERVATISM

The post–World War I years also brought new growth to the AFL and other unions. In 1918 alone, the federation grew by 40 percent, to a substantial 3.3 million members. The United Mine Workers hit the half-million mark, with the vast majority of its members being coal miners. By the following year, nearly 2 million railroad laborers had either joined the AFL or some other labor organization. With such numbers, the years 1919–1922 saw a plethora of strikes, 10,000 in all, that involved at least 8 million workers. Strikes were common and everywhere, it seemed:

> Strikes rolled through California citrus fields, southern cotton mills . . . silk mills, New England telephone companies . . . pulp and paper mills, El Paso laundries, Arizona cotton fields, Tampa cigar factories, even the Boston police force. In February 1919, a general strike in Seattle mobilized 100,000 workers, including AFL members, independent unions of Japanese butchers,

railroad workers and others, and unorganized workers. They ran Seattle for five entirely peaceful days, calling off the strike when troops dispatched to "restore order" were nearing the city.[115]

After World War I, however, a new conservatism was to descend across the United States. Many Americans became concerned about the influence of radicals, socialists, and anarchists. The Russians had successfully carried out a socialist revolution and established a form of Marxist Communism in place of their hated ruler, the tsar. The U.S. Justice Department established, in 1920, a Radical Division, with a young J. Edgar Hoover at its helm. Soon the government was carrying out raids against alleged radicals and Communist sympathizers. In a domino fashion, by 1921, 32 state legislatures outlawed "criminal syndicalism," and its advocacy of illegal labor practices and the encouragement of radicalism. In 1923, the state of California alone convicted more than 160 IWW members and Communists, sending them to prison. The unions fought back by the only means they knew—strikes. Huge strikes were carried out in 1922 by textile workers, railroad laborers, and coal miners, but many of the gains made in the post–World War I years were gone. The following year, America's union membership had tumbled to 3.6 million. Within the AFL, membership was down by one-fourth.

In addition, three big labor leaders died within a few years of the end of the Great War. Gompers died in 1924 while in Mexico City attending the Fourth Congress of the Pan-American Federation of Labor (PAFL). Debs passed away on October 20, 1926. He had last run as the Socialist Party candidate for president in 1920. (At the time, he was again in prison, so he ran as "Prisoner 9653," taking 900,000 votes.) By the year of his death, membership in the SP was only 8,000. The Wobblies' leader, Bill Haywood, struggling with diabetes, left the United States for the Communist-controlled Soviet Union, where he died on May 18, 1928. His International Workers of the World was in fragments with few members, after many were put out of work by the mechanization of labor in the mining, timber, and longshore industries.

LABOR LEFT OUT

The 1920s, then, proved to be a difficult decade for labor unions in the United States. This was the case, even as the nation's economy expanded in spectacular ways. The boom market of the "Roaring Twenties" would be based on high profits for businesses, and their investors, as well as further industrialization of the nation's economy. From 1924 to the end of the decade, the auto and steel industries saw a 50 percent increase in production. Other fields, such as chemicals and electrical equipment, grew by an even greater margin. Corporate profits soared by 50 percent, from $7.6 billion in 1924 to $11.7 billion by 1929. The nation's economic vitality was both driven and dependent on the power of a few hundred giant corporations, such as U.S. Steel, General Motors, Westinghouse Electric, and Anaconda Copper. Two hundred such corporate giants produced more profit than the nation's remaining top 300,000 businesses combined. There were great bank mergers, and stock prices flew sky-high, with investors and speculators reaping handsome dividends.

A significant number of America's workers also gained by this economic whirlwind. Wages rose steadily through most of the 1920s, even as food and other daily costs remained relatively flat. Consumer credit was easy—perhaps too easy—to get, allowing consumers to purchase industrial goods—phonographs, automobiles, cameras, vacuum cleaners, clothing, and countless other household and domestic items, whether they could afford them or not.

For the nation's labor movement, however, the struggle was still an uphill climb. Fat-cat corporations, together with sympathetic government allies, such as judges, police, and elected legislators, redoubled their efforts to undercut unions. Nearly 1,000 labor injunctions were issued during the decade, and police arrests of strikers remained a routine matter. Authorities arrested nearly 7,500 workers during a single 1926 garment workers' strike in New York City. Even labor leaders themselves, including those who headed the AFL and the railroad brotherhoods, were less radical and sometimes even fairly conservative, "renouncing militancy and giving up on efforts to organize the unorganized."[116] Samuel Gompers's successor at the helm of the AFL, William Green, found massive strikes almost impossible to organize, considering what he called the "appalling indifference of the workers themselves."[117] There were even those in the United States who felt that perhaps the labor movement was dead, killed off by a greater national prosperity and worker apathy. Between 1923 and 1929, union membership in the United States fell from 3.6 million members to 3.4 million. The United Mine Workers, whose membership boasted a half million in 1920, could only count 84,000 members by 1929.

Founding the CIO

Despite its many setbacks, the labor movement would not lie down and die. By the end of the 1920s, the nation's boom times were over, and the country slipped into a massive economic depression. It seemed to begin with the collapse of the stock market in the fall of 1929, but that crash was only a symptom of an economy that had hinged too much on the automobile and housing industries, the market's overvalued stocks, and the assumption that many Americans were economically better off than they actually were. After adjustment was made for inflation, average real wages had only risen one percent annually from 1923 to 1929. In some places and in some cases, wages actually declined for American workers, especially those in the textile, leather, glass, tobacco, and mining industries. Wages for many anthracite coal miners dropped by 14 percent from 1923 to the end of the decade. Only 1 out of every 20 American households actually had personal stockbrokers. About 30 percent of the nation's annual income had been going to only 5 percent of American families.

By May 1933, just weeks into Franklin D. Roosevelt's term as president, labor delivered its next spirited attack. A large-scale strike took place in St. Louis when 1,400 women, three out of four of them black, began a work stoppage after wage cuts at local nut-shelling factories. They were members of the Food Workers Industrial Union. With support from other unions, the female workers won their strike after less than two weeks. Spurred on by their example, other strikes soon took place, and during the last six months of the year, more than three-quarters of a million laborers joined a union, an extremely high number, at the lowest point of the depression. By the end of 1934, AFL membership passed 3 million, better than its supporters prior to 1929. By the mid-1930s, one out of every three union members belonged to an industrial union, twice the percentage before the original stock market crash.

RECOGNITION OF THE RIGHT TO EXIST

During the Great Depression of the 1930s, the U.S. economy experienced downward trends that brought great misery on the country's population. In response, President Franklin Roosevelt chose to use the government in new ways to fight the Depression and help the nation recover. The general package of legislation created by the Roosevelt administration and the U.S. Congress was called the New Deal. Acts were passed to help as many sectors of the economy as possible. There were job programs, direct relief programs, programs for the elderly, for farmers, banks, corporations, and homeowners. Several acts were designed to aid the country's workers and organized labor. No act passed during the second phase of the New Deal would be more important for the labor movement, however, than one passed on July 5, 1935.

The act was sponsored by New York senator Robert Wagner and was called the National Labor Relations Act (NLRA). (It would become known popularly as the Wagner Act.) It was unquestionably prolabor. If the NLRA's Section 7(a) had recognized the right of unions to exist, the Wagner Act protected them, even if it did not include some worker types, such as agriculturalists, hospital, employees and domestic workers. The act also required the use of secret ballot elections when workers were voting on whether to be represented by a union or not.

In addition, employers could not interfere with labor organizing, and the act was sure to list the practices employers were no longer legally allowed to do to antagonize labor organizing, including "using threats, coercion, or restraint."[118] Once a union was formed in a business, the employer was required to make attempts to work with and bargain with the union. Employers were banned from discriminating against union supporters in their hiring and firing practices. Any worker reporting an employer's violations of the Wagner Act was not to be punished by his or her employer. To sum up the scope of the Wagner Act: "Nothing in this Act shall be construed so as to interfere with or impede or diminish in any way the right to strike."[119]

Passage of the NLRA seemed to provide organized labor with yet another reason to take new courage, as unions, led by the United Mine Workers, campaigned across the country with posters and sound trucks, spreading the message of the NLRA's Section 7(a): "The president wants you to join the union."[120] Some unions gained 50,000 members; others added 100,000. The AFL chartered more than 1,400 new unionized locals. Some of the new growth was generated by more radical unions, led by the Trade Union Unity League (TUUL), a left-wing rival organization formed in August 1929 that included such divergent labor groups as New Mexican coal miners, Ohio steelworkers, sharecroppers in the Mississippi Delta, beauty shop operators, gas station attendants, and Hollywood actors. (The Screen Actors Guild in Los Angeles was led by horror movie actor Boris Karloff and the zany comic Groucho Marx.)

Strikes became the driving force of organized labor, just as they had been in earlier decades. During 1933–1934, 3,500 strikes were carried out and the trend carried into 1935 with an additional 2,000. Those in agricultural lines of work often had trouble forcing their demands on employers, since minimum farm wages had not been included under the NLRA.

THE GOVERNMENT GETS INVOLVED

In the midst of these great conflicts between striking workers and businesses that fought with all their means against them, the federal government passed several positive pieces of legislation, portions of which could only be described as pro-labor. The Social Security Act, passed in 1935, established national unemployment insurance, paid for by an employer tax and administered by state governments. It also included pensions for workers, who paid into a fund through payroll taxes, along with employers. The Social Security Act was a new approach by government: "For the first time, the federal government took responsibility for working people's long-term economic security."[121] In addition to this act, Congress raised considerably the rates of federal taxes on big businesses and their wealthy owners. Legislators also passed the Public Utility Holding Company Act, which was intended to break up gas and electric utility monopolies to help reduce their high rates. The most important governmental act to have an impact on organized labor during these years, however, was the National Labor Relations Act, because it recognized the right of unions to exist.

If the first phase of the New Deal was friendlier to employers and big business, the Second New Deal era gave concessions and protections to workers. Employers, of course, despised the new law and tried to devise ways to bypass it altogether. By 1935, however, much of the die

First signed into law in July 1935, the Wagner Act protects the rights of workers to organize labor unions. Here, miners and steelworkers march down a street in Farrell, Pennsylvania, on May 1, 1937, to celebrate the Supreme Court's upholding of the act.

was cast on behalf of labor, and a new era for labor was about to begin. Optimistic workers held the Wagner Act up as a hope for the future of organized labor, even as many workers were deciding to support a move to unionize mass production. The AFL itself was split among its leadership, including "those who preferred to ignore mass-production workers entirely, and those who were willing to take in new dues-paying members as long as their own prerogatives and power remained intact."[122]

Despite the debate, the number of mass-production unions was increasing. In the fall of 1935, a new national automobile union was established and, soon afterward, a rubber union. The members of these unions were skilled workers, many of whom were concerned that unskilled workers would take their jobs, given the difficulties brought on by the Depression. When AFL leaders met at their convention in Atlantic City in October 1935, they soon found themselves fighting a challenge movement within the ranks of the Federation, led by John L. Lewis, the president of the United Mine Workers.

At one point, this struggle between industrial and craft unionists came down to a debate and vote over a resolution that called for "unrestricted industrial union charters for mass-production industries."[123] On the convention floor, hours of debate on the issue reached a fever pitch. Once a vote was taken and the move was defeated, 18,000 votes to nearly 11,000, the issue seemed finished. Both sides kept after one another, though, arguing loudly and sometimes trying to silence their opponents. At one point, John Lewis slugged William Hutcheson, the president of the carpenters' union, after Hutcheson called Lewis a "big bastard."[124]

A UNION FOR THE UNSKILLED

As the convention stretched into the following month, Lewis and seven additional AFL leaders met on November 9 and took a bold step. They established in one stroke a new labor organization, the Committee for Industrial Organization (CIO; it later became the Congress of Industrial Organizations). They stated their intent was "for the purpose of encouraging and promoting the organization of unorganized workers . . . on an industrial basis."[125] Lewis and the others who brought the CIO to life represented unions that had been active for many years, including the United Mine Workers (UMW); Amalgamated Clothing Workers; Ladies' Garment Workers; Mine, Mill, and Smelter Workers; United Textile Workers, Cap and Millinery Workers; and Oil and Gas Workers.

Pushing this new organization was yet another redirection for the American labor movement. The Great Depression had caused a grassroots drive that had resulted in the passage of the Wagner Act. Now, those same elements were attempting to bring about change within the movement, and the CIO could take its first steps with confidence without the cooperation of the AFL. (For the moment, the CIO technically remained within the ranks of the AFL, although the AFL did not sanction the actions taken later by John L. Lewis to organize strikes of CIO member unions.) That confidence sprang from the jump in membership in the UMW and in the garment unions. Those new dues-paying members, hundreds of thousands of them, had provided what could only be called "seed money" for the CIO.

The CIO was a labor union initially formed from eight unions, with a membership of 1 million strong. The growth of the CIO would prove phenomenal. After its first two years in existence, the CIO included 32 unions and a membership of 3.7 million, almost all of whom were covered by collective bargaining contracts. (By comparison, the AFL could claim only 3.4 million.) Most of the new organization's members were employed in mass production and industrial unions. Among the CIO's largest membership were the Steel Workers Organizing Committee (later the United Steel Workers of America), with more than 500,000 members; the UMW's 600,000 members; and the United Auto Workers and United Rubber Workers (375,000 workers each). The latter two had jumped ship from the AFL to join the CIO. Another 1.3 million members were employed in the textile, garment, electrical, transportation, retail, and office-based worker industries.

The contrasts and comparisons between the older AFL and the newly formed CIO need to be examined. Among the similarities, both the AFL and the CIO member unions were supporters of collective bargaining. As with the AFL, CIO leaders basically "preferred to act as labor generals who led their troops in battle, not as temporarily elected representatives who reflected the wishes of the ranks."[126] The CIO was established with different strategies in mind, however. From the outset, the new organization was nearly color-blind on behalf of racial unity among its members. The CIO also courted America's immigrant populations, both new and old, and was much more directly involved in politics. With Franklin D. Roosevelt in the White House, the CIO felt it had a friend in power and gave its support to FDR during his reelection bid in 1936. Because of the supportive efforts of John Lewis's UMW and other CIO organizations, Roosevelt garnered millions of working-class votes. The CIO would come to be seen as a labor organization with which to reckon.

A HIGH-PROFILE ORGANIZATION

It would be the Rubber Workers who would draw national attention to the CIO first. A few hundred workers in Akron, Ohio, struck the Goodyear tire plant in February 1936, when the company announced layoffs. Before week's end, 14,000 additional Goodyear employees went out on strike in support. Soon, there were enough striking workers to form a circle around the tire plant that stretched 11 miles (17.7 kilometers). Even when heavy snows fell, the workers came out and walked the picket lines. When Goodyear officials managed to get an injunction against the strikers, the URW and others threatened a wider, general strike. With every step the company tried, a larger labor force threatened to expand the strike. Here was labor marching in coordinated fashion with large numbers at their disposal, remaining unbowed by management's challenges. Within a few weeks, tire company officials agreed to the workers' demands.

The CIO achieved even greater successes in 1937. Through a successful "sit-down" strike by UAW in Detroit and Flint, Michigan, the labor organization gained recognition by General Motors officials to represent its workers through contract negotiations. The "sit-down" strike was a new tactic of organized labor, where workers who struck a factory not only set up picket lines outside but simply occupied the plant to further their case and make certain the facility did not continue to produce using scab labor.

THE GREAT SIT-DOWN STRIKE

By the 1930s, many of the patterns and practices established by organized labor had already been tested over and over for their efficiency and power to bring about change. During the mid-1930s, however, labor organizers pulled off a new twist on the old labor standby—the strike.

By the fall of 1936, an important group of workers—the United Automobile Workers (UAW), numbering 300,000 strong—began to take steps in an effort to be recognized by some of the largest corporations in the United States, those in the auto industry. The UAW had come into existence through a combination of federal unions brought together by the AFL. When the automakers continued to ignore them, however, UAW officials chose to leave the AFL in 1936 and join the CIO. They then elected a new president, the "young and idealistic" Homer S. Martin.[127] Martin's climb, however, was uphill from the start.

At the time, three powerhouses dominated the field of automobile building—Ford, Chrysler, and General Motors. Despite the Wagner Act, which required businesses to recognize and agree to work with unions, the big three automakers had refused to work with the UAW or make concessions when they made demands. Autoworkers had grown tired of waiting. Many worked 60- to 70-hour weeks

In 1936, Homer S. Martin was named president of the United Automobile Workers (UAW). The former Protestant minister advocated sit-down strikes to gain recognition from the automobile manufacturers. Martin (center) is pictured here with fellow labor leaders John Brophy (left) and John L. Lewis.

for wages as low as 20¢ an hour. They were forced to fill weekly quotas through a despised "speedup system," which might require three workers to perform the work previously done by four. Frequently, plant managers spied on their workers and fired any they discovered involved in any union activity. "We don't want to be driven," became the mantra of the thousands who built America's cars, "we don't want to be spied on."[128] UAW President Martin, when making overtures to the executive officers of General Motors concerning collective bargaining, was patronizingly told to have his workers talk to their plant managers if they had grievances.

Even before Martin and the UAW could officially decide on their next plan of action, union organizers at a GM plant in Detroit, Michigan, took matters into their own hands. Just days after Christmas, on the evening of December 30, a group of autoworkers suddenly took control of the floor of the plant where they worked, GM's Fisher Plant No. 2. The next day, workers at another GM facility, Fisher No. 1, in Flint, decided during their lunch break to follow suit, as a few hundred plant workers approached the factory guards and plant managers and led them out of the facility. Closing the doors behind them, the factory workers did not intend to establish picket lines outside the factory. They were engaging in a new type of work stoppage—the sit-down strike.

It was not the first time the sit-down had been used as a labor tactic, but it was employed previously only on a limited scale. The UAW workers were prepared to put the sit-down strike to the test. The approach was a simple one: Rather than put themselves outside the facility on a picket line and allow owners to continue to use their plant productively by employing replacement or scab labor, the workers occupied the plant itself, effectively shutting down operation. They literally sat down on work benches or even on automobile seats that had not yet been installed. Unlike many earlier labor tactics, which had frequently led to violence, the sit-down strike functioned as a form of nonviolent labor resistance.

Once this strike began, support spread quickly throughout the neighboring auto-producing towns of Flint and Detroit. Plant officials claimed the sit-down was an illegal violation of property rights and made demands that the strikers be driven from the factory floors. Martin, however, shrewdly countered their claim: "What more sacred property right is there in the world today than the right of a man to his job? The property right involves the right to support his family, feed his children and keep starvation away from the door."[129]

CIO leader John Lewis gave his hearty support to the striking workers. "You men are undoubtedly carrying on through one of the most heroic battles that has ever been undertaken by strikers in an industrial dispute. The attention of the entire American public is focused upon you."[130] Indeed, Americans were watching, listening to what was taking place in Flint and Detroit, where the strikers stubbornly refused to leave their factory fortresses, even after factory officials cut off the plant's heat. More attention was turned to their cause when police attempted to assault Fisher Body Plant No. 2. Strikers lobbed anything they could get their hands on—"coffee mugs, pop bottles, iron bolts, and heavy automobile door hinges"—and sent the police reeling back.[131] A second police attack included tear gas, as the strikers turned factory fire hoses on them, again sending the law enforcers scattering, a retreat the workers would later refer to as the "Battle of the Running Bulls."[132]

Frustrated factory officials watched as the strike dragged on week after week. The strikers received food from the outside, often delivered in picnic baskets by their wives. The strikers constantly patrolled the factory, which the workers kept brightly lit to watch for possible attacks from the police or other strikebreakers. During the strike, no alcohol was permitted inside the plant. Some of the workers slept in the bodies of cars still on the plant assembly line. Many of the workers decided not to shave until they had won their strike.

In desperation, company officials finally asked Michigan's Governor Frank Murphy to order state militia to be called out to force an end to the strike. Murphy refused, however, fearing bloodshed. (He was also sympathetic to the striking autoworkers.) Then, GM officers managed to get a court order against the strikers, which called for the strike to end at 3 P.M. on February 3. All workers failing to

The Flint, Michigan, sit-down strike of December 1936 through February 1937 made the UAW a household name and ultimately led to the unionization of the auto industry. Here, strikers guard the windows of General Motors' Fisher Body plant in Flint during the strike.

comply could face fines and possible prison. The strikers, however, would not budge, telegraphing Governor Murphy: "Unarmed as we are, the introduction of the militia . . . will mean a blood-bath of unarmed workers. . . . We have decided to stay in the plant."[133]

Greatly concerned, Governor Murphy ordered all involved parties to sit down with him and work out an agreement. John Lewis agreed, and so did GM Vice President William Knudsen. February 3 arrived, however, with no agreement. With the strikers inside the plant heavily barricaded and ready for an assault they were certain would come, and thousands of workers outside manning the picket lines, Governor Murphy stood his ground and refused to order in the militia, in defiance of the court order. Then, the following day, President Roosevelt intervened, asking all sides to continue their talks. After a week of negotiations, GM officials finally agreed to recognize the United Automobile Workers and empower them to negotiate all future contracts and not to discriminate against union members. The victory for the UAW was sweet: It marked the first time the CIO had managed to gain an agreement from an open-shop industry and from one of the world's largest corporations. It would put the automobile industry on the road to complete unionization, all because a small group of workers had chosen to leave their jobs, but not their workplace, and sit down.

THE AFTERMATH OF THE "SIT-DOWN" STRIKE

That victory of February 1937 was followed the next month by another, this time in the steel industry. After officials at U.S. Steel watched the UAW launch its "sit-down" strike, with Michigan's governor refusing to send in state militia troops to break the strike even under threat of a court order, they decided to sit down themselves with John L. Lewis and negotiate. Just three weeks after the UAW "sit-down" strike, the CIO signed a union-management contract with U.S. Steel, giving the labor organization bargaining power for its workers, a 10 percent wage increase, an eight-hour day, and a 40-hour workweek. Success seemed to mark the path of John L. Lewis and the CIO.

The future did not bring good news to the CIO or to many other organized labor organizations, however. The year 1937 saw the economy slide back into deep depression, despite some gains over the previous four years, in part because of Roosevelt's New Deal and more government money being pumped into the national economy. This Second Great Depression halted the recovery, hitting everyone, including the workers, hard. The UAW, fresh from its gains at Flint and Detroit, lost three of every four members. The membership of the steel and rubber workers unions also declined significantly. Although some CIO-affiliated unions did see growth over the next two years, overall membership declined by several hundred thousand workers.

These years brought retrenchment to the CIO and to the labor movement in general. By the spring of 1938, the Committee for Industrial Organization was renamed the Congress of Industrial Organizations, which was formed completely independently of the AFL's superstructure. Relations between the AFL and CIO had soured, especially after the Federation expelled all CIO unions from among its ranks in 1937. The AFL took a strong position against the CIO during the late 1930s, labeling its rival, as one AFL union leader described it, as a "gang of sluggers, communists, radicals and soapbox artists, professional bums, expelled members of labor unions, outright scabs and the Jewish organizations with all their red affiliates."[134] The CIO's bad reputation began to take its toll. While AFL membership grew from 3.4 to 4 million members from 1937 through 1939, the CIO slipped in membership by hundreds of thousands to half the membership of the AFL, causing the organization's leaders to abandon such confrontational tactics as the sit-down strike, despite its earlier successes.

9

Labor's Struggle Continues

The 1940s ushered in a new era for America's organized labor. During the 1940 Presidential election, both the AFL and the CIO gave their support publicly to the Democrats and the reelection of Franklin D. Roosevelt to a third term. In that election, perhaps as many as 75 percent of their members voted for FDR. Despite this support for the president, John L. Lewis did oppose the president's reelection, calling it "a national evil of the first magnitude."[135] Lewis was disappointed in the lack of success of the New Deal and blamed FDR for the nation's lack of recovery. His stance against the president's reelection cost him dearly. He had miscalculated his influence over CIO members and their votes and had not only taken himself completely out of politics but had also sacrificed control of the organization that he had done so much to build up. He would soon lose his leadership of the CIO. The new CIO president would be Philip Murray. Lewis still remained at the helm of the United Mine Workers, however, and he chose to lead them out of the CIO and rejoin them with the AFL.

When the flames of war finally engulfed the United States following the Japanese attack on Pearl Harbor in December 1941, the labor movement would see significant rises in domestic production on behalf of the war effort. With this turn in the U.S. economy, workers found their wages increasing. Skilled workers were in constant demand for wartime production. Overall, American workers' wartime wages increased by 20 percent. Gone were the days of the Depression, "as union members and wage earners shared substantially in the mounting profits of wartime business."[136]

Unfortunately for Lewis, he made yet another misstep, this time during the war. In 1943, at the height of the war, Lewis called for a strike by the United Mine Workers for higher wages. The public response to the strike was profoundly negative. Such a move was even considered unpatriotic. Roosevelt responded to Lewis's call for a strike by appealing to the miners directly, through a radio address, telling them that any miner who stopped his work would be hurting the war effort. "Tomorrow the Stars and Stripes will fly over the coal mines," said the president. "I hope every miner will be at work under that flag."[137] So much hatred was pointed at Lewis that, when *Fortune* magazine published a questionnaire in November 1943 that included the question, "Are there any prominent individuals in this country who you feel might be harmful to the future of the country unless they are curbed?" 36 percent of the responses mentioned John L. Lewis. (The next-closest name was FDR, who polled only 3 percent.) Another problem for Lewis was the support his labor organizations received from Communists. Although Lewis and other top labor bosses were Democrats and anti-Communist, they did not consider Communists in the United States as a threat to the country. For Lewis, as long as the Communist Party of America gave its support to the CIO, he welcomed their support. This approach did not sit well with some Americans.

FDR certainly benefited from the political support he received from both the AFL and the CIO. At the same time, Roosevelt was anxious to have the AFL and the CIO rejoin their ranks, a call he first made in 1937. He needed support from organized labor and believed it was "greatly to his interest to have a united movement strong enough to rally the progressive forces of the nation behind his policies."[138]

Talks between the two organizations did take place from time to time in the late 1930s, but nothing was achieved. Basically, while the issues of craft unions versus industrial unions no longer had any real purpose, the leaders of both groups were not willing to surrender power by reuniting with their rival organization.

Despite the ongoing rivalry and ups and downs experienced by the AFL and the CIO, as well as with other union organizations, the handwriting was on the wall for organized labor. Union membership may have hit its highest levels during the years prior to World War II (1941–1945). Strikes, naturally, were typically avoided, in part because a special government agency, the War Labor Board (WLB), remained in the middle of many labor disputes. Throughout the war, the WLB forced settlements in nearly 18,000 labor cases, which in turn affected more than 12 million workers. Nineteen out of 20 times, the WLB's involvement was able to avoid strikes that disrupted production. An additional whopping 415,000 voluntary wage agreements involved about 20 million workers. Even though labor and management constantly criticized the policies of the WLB, they accepted them the vast majority of the time, with neither side wishing to be thought of as unpatriotic. President Roosevelt himself only had to step in directly and take action in about two dozen cases. By the war's end, the War Labor Board had proven itself to be one of the most successful wartime agencies. As the labor historian Philip Taft has described this governmental body, its performance "was one of the more notable accomplishments of a government agency dealing with economic problems during World War II."[139]

The War Labor Board (WLB) was established by President Woodrow Wilson in 1918 to ensure that major labor disputes did not escalate into strikes. During World War II, the WLB was responsible for forcing the settlement of nearly 18,000 labor cases. Here, AFL president William Green (left) meets with CIO president Philip Murray (right) and War Production Board Chairman Donald M. Nelson to discuss potential labor-management disputes that might hinder the U.S. war effort.

LABOR FOLLOWING THE WAR

Following the war, unions struggled to keep their share of influence over the nation's labor force. For many workers, the reasons for which earlier labor unions had been formed were no longer of interest or problematic. Throughout the first half of the twentieth century, the typical American workplace experienced change, including better working conditions, better employer-employee relations, increased responsiveness on the part of management, better pay, and better hours. In short, for many workers it began to appear that labor unions had served their purpose and, for some, had outlived their usefulness. Although labor organizations had always struggled with popularly perceived images (they were often described as nests of radicals, anarchists, socialists, and other militant and far-left groups), during the 1940s and 1950s, those perceptions continued to survive. In addition, those decades saw more and more links between organized labor and organized crime, which only further hurt the popular image of unions.

Labor organizations also suffered a setback after the war, when, in 1947, Congress passed the Taft-Hartley Act. The act made modifications on the Wagner Act that had become law during the 1930s. It came about in part because of criticism of some labor groups and their activities both during and just after the war. Complaints regarded wartime coal strikes and strikes in the steel, auto, and other industries, including the railroad industry, after the war. In 1946, a rail strike threatened to close down the struggling postwar economy. These labor stoppages were seen by the American people as having hampered the war and damaged the postwar economy. While it was working its way through Congress as a bill, the Taft-Hartley proposal was roundly denounced by the labor unions. President Harry Truman (FDR had died suddenly in office, in April 1945) vetoed it, referring to it as a "slave labor bill," yet it was passed by Congress.[140]

Another act was passed by Congress just four years later that placed additional restrictions and requirements on America's labor organizations. The Labor-Management Reporting and Disclosure Act (known as the Landrum-Griffin Act) was passed in 1959. This act placed financial disclosure and fiduciary responsibility on all pension and welfare fund administrators, including those connected with organized labor. The act also included a "Worker's Bill of Rights," which stated in detail what all unions were required to provide for

THE TAFT-HARTLEY ACT

The Taft-Hartley Act of 1947, known officially as the Labor-Management Relations Act, was created by a senator, Robert Taft, and a member of the House of Representatives, Fred Hartley. By amending the Wagner Act (National Labor Relations Act of 1935), this new law created a list of unfair labor practices, those carried out by the unions. By comparison, the National Labor Relations Act of 1935 had generally only listed unfair practices by employers. The Taft-Hartley banned jurisdictional strikes, which occur when a union strikes to put pressure on an employer to assign specific work to that union's employees. The act also prohibited secondary boycotts and "common situs" picketing, which occurs when unions strike or refuse to handle the products of a business with which the strikers have no specific argument simply because that business is connected to the business being initially targeted by a labor stoppage. (In 1959, another such act, the Labor-Management Reporting and Disclosure Act, would place even more restrictions on secondary boycotts.)

The act placed additional limits on organized labor. It banned closed shops (agreements that limited an employer to hiring only union members), which had become increasingly common by the 1940s. Also, unions would be held responsible for strike-related damages. Strikes by federal employees were banned, and the law authorized the president of the United States to issue 80-day injunctions when strikes raise a threat concerning national health and safety. Although popular sentiment across the country had helped push the Taft-Hartley Act into reality, labor organizations were angered by its restrictions. Not one labor leader approved of the Taft-Hartley Act. When it was passed, the UAW closed down automobile plants for five symbolic hours in support of a massive rally in Detroit against the act. The act, however, was here to stay.

their members, including a copy of the union contract under which each worker was employed. The act also required unions to establish standards for electing union officers and for disciplining local organizations. Landrum-Griffin also banned all convicted felons and Communists from holding a union office until they had been out of prison for a minimum of five years or out of the Communist Party for that same length of time. Although the AFL-CIO already desired that union funds be regulated and had previously taken steps to keep convicted felons and even former Communists from union office, then AFL-CIO President George Meany condemned Landrum-Griffin as "government interference in union business."[141]

UNIONS AND RACE ISSUES

The 1960s appear to have placed the American labor movement at a crossroads. Many of the earlier goals of better working conditions and better pay had already been addressed, but not for everyone. For some workers during this tumultuous decade, "organizing unions was a civil rights struggle."[142] Some minority workers found themselves segregated out of the mainstream of the labor movement and fought to gain recognition. For example, New York City hospital workers were nearly all black and Puerto Rican women. They did not receive federal labor law protection, were not allowed to strike according to state law, and typically were paid less than standard wages. As early as 1958, New York's Hospital and Health Care Workers Local 1199 began organizing these female, minority workers and, by the following year, had won a 46-day strike that resulted in better pay and benefits. By 1962, hospital workers struck again, this time gaining recognition of their union from hospital managements. Other minority hospital workers followed suit throughout the decade.

Farmworkers were another labor group who, even by the early 1960s, were not covered by the protections of the

During the summer of 1981, federal air traffic controllers went on strike in support of better wages and working conditions. Here, workers walk the picket line at the New York air route traffic control center in Ronkonkoma, New York.

Wagner Act. In 1962, Latino farm labor organizers Cesar Chavez and Dolores Huerta established the National Farm Workers Association (NFWA) in Delano, California. By the mid-1960s, the organization had 1,700 members. In 1965, Filipino grape pickers associated with the AFL-CIO called a strike in Delano and asked the NFWA to join them. Chavez agreed.

By the 1970s, union membership was both gaining and losing. Since then, union membership has been in decline in the nation's private sector, including industrial jobs, whereas it has grown in the public sector, including government contracts. During the past several decades, states have passed "Right-to-Work" laws that often deny unions the power to negotiate for groups of workers. This has generally caused labor organizations to be weaker in power and influence in states that have such laws.

The 1980s witnessed a handful of meaningful strikes with potentially far-reaching effects. In the late summer of 1981, federal air traffic controllers cooperated on a nationwide strike after their union failed to accept the U.S. government's offer for a new contract. Although the government issued a "back-to-work" order, the majority of the country's 13,000 striking air controllers continued their walkout. In response, on August 5, President Ronald Reagan, a conservative Republican leader, chose to dismiss those defiant controllers. Five years later, female airline flight attendants finally won an 18-year-old lawsuit, *United Airlines, Inc. v. McDonald*, against United Airlines. Previous airline policy had required female flight attendants to be fired when they married. A U.S. district court approved the restatement of nearly 500 flight attendants. In addition, the airline was required to pay $37 million in back pay, as part of a settlement compensating more than 1,700 flight attendants.

Today, union membership is a minority club among workers. In recent years, American union membership in the private sector has fallen to less than 9 percent, the lowest percentage of unionism among the nation's workers since 1932. Labor unions do not hold the attraction they once had for many laborers in the United States, and many workers do not appear interested in joining. Strikes in the United States have almost become a tactic of the past. Even in sectors of the economy that have been highly unionized in earlier decades, including the auto industry and steel production, union membership has fallen, as the numbers of workers in those large-scale industries have dropped. In the major American cities, where the majority of construction workers used to be unionized, today the shift has been from 75 percent union members to fewer than one out of four. Only commercial construction has been able to keep union membership above 50 percent. Unions have struggled and continue to struggle with an inability to keep nonunionized companies from gaining construction contacts at their expense.

One important factor that has redefined the landscape for America's labor unions has been the National Labor Relations Act (NLRA) and the agency it created, the National Labor Relations Board (NLRB), part of the U.S. Department of Labor. Under the act, public-sector-worker unions are governed by the NLRB, as are the labor laws and labor boards in all 50 states. Many northern states have made a practice of designing their laws and boards to mirror those of the NLRA and NLRB. Most of those laws specify that, if a group of workers wants to join a union, they must either gain voluntary recognition for their union by their employer or have a majority of themselves, working in a "bargaining unit" to vote for union membership and representation. Outside of the northern states, however, public workers do not generally have the right to organize a union as a legal body. This has led to a hard fact for organized labor: Approximately 40 percent of public employees in the country do not have the right to organize a legally established union.

Today, American organized labor is dominated by the giant combined organization of the AFL-CIO. It is the largest federation of unions in the country and includes 53 national and international unions, which represent a combined constituency of 9 million workers. (This membership is 40 percent below the high-water mark of membership for the AFL-CIO, which was achieved when the two separate labor organizations joined forces for a second time, in 1955, when total membership was 15 million.) During the past 50 years, the AFL-CIO's member unions have represented nearly all unionized laborers in the United States, with the largest membership comprising the American Federation of State, County, and Municipal Employees (AFSCME), which has a membership of more than 1 million workers.

As American labor moves through the first decade of the twenty-first century, a significant amount of uncertainty stalks the movement. Taking the long view of the history of the movement, the American worker has much to be proud of. For so many decades, throughout the nineteenth century and much of the twentieth, the movement was key to redefining the relationship between those who worked "by the sweat of their brow," as the Knights of Labor had described them, and those who owned and operated the nation's mills, factories, mines, railroads, and other workplaces. It was organized labor that typically fought the good fight through that century and a half of intensive labor agitation and desperate union organization to create more of a level playing field for the laborers, both skilled and unskilled. Nearly every major, positive change that has brought improvement to the world of work in the United States was accomplished by labor organizations.

Historian Priscilla Murolo sums up those accomplishments:

> From the hours and conditions of labor to the regulation of occupational safety and health, to social welfare like minimum living standards for old and young or equal opportunity, even the democratic franchise itself, many aspects of everyday life show the results of working people organized to advance their common interests. Despite these advances, the struggles never seem to end. Working people have returned again and again to the same issues of economic security and political democracy, though under new and changing conditions.[143]

Today, modern American workers, many of whom labor in an increasingly mechanized or technologically plugged-in workplace, seem so far removed from the workplaces of 1865 or 1894 or 1937, when labor organizations fought hard for even basic recognition and ethical treatment by those who employed them. Those earlier generations of workers, however, whether they were unskilled Ohio canal laborers, Philadelphia cordwainers, Washington, D.C., typographers, Colorado miners, Pittsburgh steelworkers, New York cigar makers, Chicago railroad employees, Detroit automobile workers, or California fruit pickers, helped to lay the groundwork for organized labor. Workers in each generation stood on the shoulders of those who came before them, and each helped to create, for the vast majority of today's workers, safe work environments where they may labor knowing they will be paid for their worth.

CHRONOLOGY

1636	A group of Maine fishermen protests to their employer after he withholds their wages.
1741	Journeyman Caulkers of Boston established to provide a united front to make demands on the craftsmen who employ them.
1768	New York journeymen tailors engage in a "turn-out," a work protest similar to the modern-day strike.
1778	New York printers demand increased wages.
1792	Philadelphia shoemakers create an early form of a labor union.
1794	New York printers create a permanent labor organization they call a "Typographical Society"; workers establish the Federal Society of Journeymen Cordwainers, one of the first trade unions of wageworkers established in the United States.
1799	The Philadelphia Cordwainers union engages in a strike and a picket of masters' shops.
1806–1815	Cordwainers Conspiracy Cases are tried, resulting in a legal decision establishing workers who band together in common cause to make demands as a "criminal conspiracy."
1827	Mechanics' Union of Trade Associations is established in Philadelphia, constituting the first U.S. labor organization to include workers from more than one trade or craft.
1831–1836	At least 200 trade associations established during these years with total membership of more than 100,000.

1834   Umbrella labor organization, the National Trades Union, is established.

1835   Largest of the federation strikes of this period takes place in Philadelphia, where 17 different craft unions give their support to striking Irish laborers who unload coal barges, marking the first general strike in U.S. history and resulting in 10-hour days for workers.

1840   Federal government passes legislation establishing a 10-hour workday for workers engaged in federal construction projects.

1842   Supreme Court decision *Commonwealth v. Hunt*, establishes legal right of workers to organize and engage in strikes if the reason is "useful and honorable."

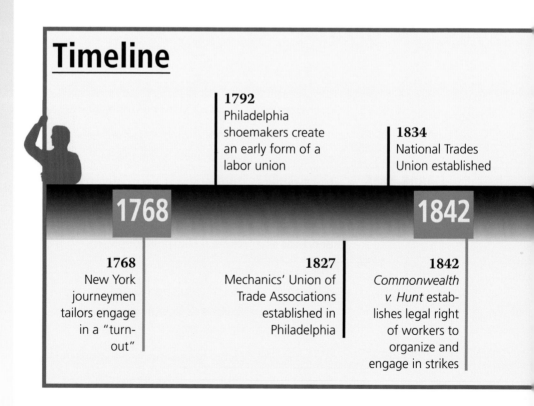

Timeline

1792
Philadelphia shoemakers create an early form of a labor union

1834
National Trades Union established

1768

1842

1768
New York journeymen tailors engage in a "turn-out"

1827
Mechanics' Union of Trade Associations established in Philadelphia

1842
Commonwealth v. Hunt establishes legal right of workers to organize and engage in strikes

1863–1864   During these years of the Civil War, the number of trade unions increases from 79 to 270, with a total membership of 200,000.

1866   National Labor Union is established.

1869   The Noble and Holy Order of the Knights of Labor is established.

1870   United States has 30 national labor organizations representing 300,000 workers.

1877   Nine Irish miners, known as the "Molly Maguires," are hanged after they organize a strike; that same year, the Great Railroad Strike is crushed.

1881–1884   Knights of Labor averages approximately 450 strikes annually.

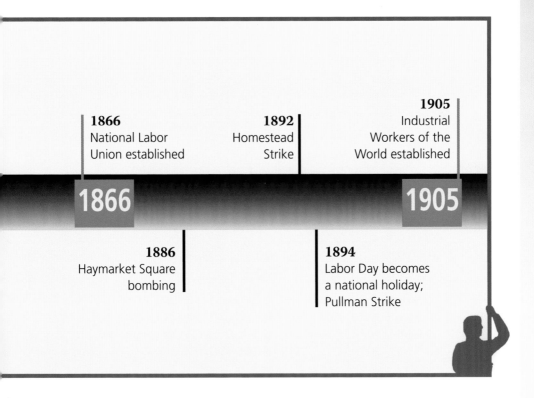

1866
National Labor
Union established

1892
Homestead
Strike

1905
Industrial
Workers of the
World established

1866

1905

1886
Haymarket Square
bombing

1894
Labor Day becomes
a national holiday;
Pullman Strike

1882   Federation of Organized Trades and Labor Unions, a collective of national craft unions is established.

1886   Knights of Labor strikes against the McCormick Harvesting Machine Company, which leads to Haymarket Square bombing; American Federation of Labor is established with Samuel Gompers as its leader.

1886–1888   Knights of Labor membership drops from 750,000 to 220,000.

1892   AFL membership stands at 250,000; the Homestead Strike is launched by an AFL-affiliated union against a steel mill owned by steel magnate Andrew Carnegie.

1893   Illinois becomes one of the first states to pass labor laws to protect children and women.

1935 The National labor Relations Act (also known as the Wagner Act) is passed	**1938** Congress creates the Fair Labor Standards Act	**1947** Congress passes the Taft-Hartley Act

1914 — **1947**

1914 U.S. Congress passes the Clayton Act	**1937** CIO leads successful "sit-down" strike at General Motors automobile plants in Detroit and Flint, Michigan

1894   Labor Day becomes a national holiday; that year also witnesses the Pullman Strike in Chicago, which leads to a national railroad strike.

1901   A rival to the AFL, the Socialist Party, is established.

1904   AFL boasts 1.67 million members in 120 union groups, a doubling of member unions compared to 1897; the National Child Labor Committee is formed to establish standards for child labor.

1905   Industrial Workers of the World is established.

1909   IWW wins a strike against a U.S. Steel-owned Pennsylvania company.

1909–1910   Socialist Party organizes a widespread strike in New York involving the Ladies Garment Workers."

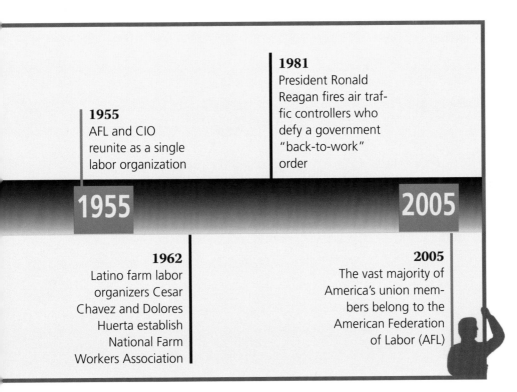

1955
AFL and CIO reunite as a single labor organization

1981
President Ronald Reagan fires air traffic controllers who defy a government "back-to-work" order

1955

2005

1962
Latino farm labor organizers Cesar Chavez and Dolores Huerta establish National Farm Workers Association

2005
The vast majority of America's union members belong to the American Federation of Labor (AFL)

1912	IWW win another work stoppage, known as the "Bread and Roses Strike," which involves 25,000 textile workers in Lawrence, Massachusetts.
1913–1914	AFL-affiliated United Mine Workers engage in widespread strike in southeastern Colorado that ends in Ludlow Massacre near Trinidad.
1914	U.S. Congress passes the Clayton Act, which affirms that labor unions must not be "construed to be illegal combinations in restraint of trade under the antitrust laws."
1919–1922	At least 10,000 work strikes take place in the United States during these years.
1924	AFL leader Samuel Gompers dies.
1923–1929	Union membership in the United States falls from 3.6 million members to 3.4 million.
1926	Police arrest 7,500 workers during a single garment workers' strike in New York City.
1933–1934	Thirty-five hundred strikes are carried out in the United States.
1935	The National Labor Relations Act (also known as the Wagner Act) is passed, which recognizes the right of labor unions to exist; John L. Lewis, president of the United Mine Workers, helps establish the Committee for Industrial Organization (CIO).
1936	Workers successfully strike against the Goodyear tire plant in Akron, Ohio.
1937	CIO leads successful "sit-down" strike at General Motors automobile plants in Detroit and Flint, Michigan.
1938	U.S. Congress creates the Fair Labor Standards Act, which places restrictions on the employment

of children; the CIO is renamed the Congress of Industrial Organizations.

1941–1945 The War Labor Board, a U.S. government agency, forces settlements in nearly 18,000 wartime labor cases, directly affecting 12 million workers.

1943 John L. Lewis leads a strike among his United Mine Workers during World War II.

1947 Congress passes the Taft-Hartley Act (officially, the Labor-Management Relations Act), which modifies the Wagner Act, placing restrictions on American labor unions.

1955 AFL and CIO reunite as a single labor organization.

1959 Congress passes the Labor Management Reporting and Disclosure Act, which places more restrictions on labor.

1962 Latino farm labor organizers Cesar Chavez and Dolores Huerta establish the National Farm Workers Association in Delano, California.

1970s Many states pass "Right-to-Work" laws, which sometimes deny unions the power to negotiate for groups of workers.

1981 President Ronald Reagan fires air traffic controllers who defy a government "back-to-work" order.

1986 Flight attendants win lawsuit, *United Airlines, Inc. v. McDonald* over UA policy of firing attendants who marry.

2005 The vast majority of America's union members belong to the American Federation of Labor (AFL).

NOTES

CHAPTER 1

1. Allen Weinstein, *Freedom and Crisis: An American History* (New York: Random House, 1974), 474.
2. Ibid., 475–476.
3. Ibid., 476.
4. Ibid., 477.
5. Ibid., 478–79.
6. James Green, *Death in the Haymarket: A Story of Chicago, the First Labor Movement and the Bombing That Divided Gilded Age America* (New York: Pantheon Books, 2006), 61.
7. Ibid., 60.
8. Ibid., 61.
9. Ibid., 62.
10. Weinstein, 481.
11. Ibid., 482.

CHAPTER 2

12. Priscilla Murolo and A.B. Chitty, *From the Folks Who Brought You the Weekend: A Short, Illustrated History of Labor in the United States* (New York: New Press, 2001), 14.
13. Ibid.
14. Ibid., 22.
15. Ibid.
16. Foster Rhea Dulles and Melvyn Dubofsky, *Labor in America, A History* (Arlington Heights, Ill.: Harlan Davidson, 1984), 14.
17. Ibid., 18.
18. Ibid., 19.
19. Murolo, 44.

CHAPTER 3

20. Ibid., 20.
21. Joseph G. Rayback, *A History of American Labor* (New York: Free Press, 1966), 54.
22. Ibid., 55.
23. Ibid., 56.
24. Dulles, 29.
25. Ibid.
26. Ibid., 30.
27. Rayback, 57.
28. Ibid.
29. Ibid., 58.
30. Murolo, 61.
31. Rayback, 66.
32. Dulles, 67.
33. Ibid., 69.
34. Ibid., 67.
35. Ibid., 68.
36. Ibid.
37. Ibid., 66.
38. Ibid.
39. Murolo, 63.
40. Dulles, 66.

CHAPTER 4

41. Murolo, 65.
42. Ibid.
43. Ibid., 67.

44. Ibid.
45. Ibid.
46. Ibid.
47. Dulles, 84.
48. Ibid.
49. Ibid., 86.
50. Ibid., 86–87.
51. Ibid., 87.
52. Ibid., 88.
53. Quoted in Murolo, 99.
54. Ibid.
55. Ibid., 104.
56. Ibid., 105.
57. Ibid., 110.
58. Ibid.

CHAPTER 5

59. Ibid., 90.
60. Ibid., 91.
61. Murolo, 111.
62. Ibid., 116.
63. Milton Meltzer, *Bread and Roses: The Struggle of American Labor, 1865–1915* (New York: Alfred A. Knopf, 1967), 101.
64. Ibid., 122.
65. Ibid.
66. Ibid., 123.
67. Ibid., 125.
68. Ibid.
69. Murolo, 126.
70. Ibid.
71. Ibid.

CHAPTER 6

72. Murolo, 128.
73. Ibid.
74. Dulles, 153–154.
75. Ibid., 154.
76. Ibid.
77. Ibid., 155.

78. Ibid., 156.
79. Ibid.
80. Ibid.
81. Ibid.
82. Ibid., 158.
83. Ibid., 162.
84. Ibid.
85. Ibid.
86. Ibid.
87. Ibid.
88. Ibid.
89. Ibid., 164.
90. Green, 130.
91. Murolo, 131.
92. Ibid., 131.
93. Rosemary Laughlin, *The Pullman Strike of 1894: American Labor Comes of Age* (Greensboro, N.C.: Morgan Reynolds, 2000), 35–36.
94. Murolo, 133.
95. Ibid.
96. Laughlin, 45.
97. Ibid., 50.
98. Murolo, 136.
99. Ibid.

CHAPTER 7

100. Murolo, 142.
101. Ibid., 145.
102. Ibid., 15.
103. Meltzer, 199.
104. Ibid., 200.
105. Ibid., 200–201.
106. Ibid., 205.
107. Ibid., 206.
108. Ibid.
109. Ibid., 208.
110. Murolo, 150.
111. Ibid.
112. Ibid., 157.

113. Ibid.
114. Ibid.
115. Ibid., 166.
116. Ibid., 175.
117. Ibid.

CHAPTER 8

118. Murolo, 201.
119. Ibid.
120. Ibid., 195.
121. Ibid., 201.
122. Ibid., 202.
123. Ibid.
124. Ibid.
125. Ibid., 203.
126. Dulles, 288.
127. Ibid., 291.
128. Ibid.
129. Ibid., 292.
130. Ibid.

131. Ibid.
132. Ibid.
133. Ibid., 293.
134. Murolo, 215.

CHAPTER 9

135. Dulles, 310.
136. Ibid., 313.
137. Ibid., 326.
138. Ibid., 307.
139. Murolo, 332.
140. "Labor Unions in the United States." Available online at *http://en.wikipedia.org/wiki/Labor_unions_in_the_United_States*
141. Murolo, 243.
142. Ibid., 259.
143. Ibid., 331.

BIBLIOGRAPHY

Boyle, Kevin, ed. *Organized Labor and American Politics, 1894–1994*. Albany: State University of New York Press, 1998.

Brody, David. *Labor Embattled: History, Power, Rights*. Urbana: University of Illinois Press, 2005.

Buhle, Paul. *Taking Care of Business: Samuel Gompers, George Meany, Lane Kirkland, and the Tragedy of American Labor*. New York: Monthly Review Press, 1999.

Dulles, Foster Rhea, and Melvyn Dubofsky. *Labor in America, A History*. Arlington Heights, Ill.: Harlan Davidson, 1984.

Erickson, Charlotte. *American Industry and the European Immigrant*. New York: Russell & Russell, 1957.

Foner, Philip S. *History of the Labor Movement in the United States, Vol. I: From Colonial Times to the Founding of the American Federation of Labor*. New York: International, 1947.

———. *History of the Labor Movement in the United States, Vol. II: From the Founding of the American Federation of Labor to the Emergence of American Imperialism*. New York: International, 1955.

———. *History of the Labor Movement in the United States, Vol. III: The Policies and Practices of the American Federation of Labor, 1900–1909*. New York: International, 1964.

———. *Organized Labor and the Black Worker, 1619–1973*. New York: Praeger, 1974.

Green, James. *Death in the Haymarket: A Story of Chicago, the First Labor Movement, and the Bombing That Divided Gilded Age America*. New York: Pantheon Books, 2006.

Madison, Charles A. *American Labor Leaders: Personalities and Forces in the Labor Movement*. New York: Frederick Ungar, 1960.

Mandel, Bernard. *Samuel Gompers, A Biography*. Yellow Springs, Ohio: Antioch Press, 1963.

Meltzer, Milton. *Bread and Roses: The Struggle of American Labor, 1865–1915.* New York: Alfred A. Knopf, 1967.

Montgomery, David. *The Fall of the House of Labor: The Workplace, the State, and American Labor Activism, 1865–1925.* New York: Cambridge University Press, 1977.

Murolo, Priscilla, and A.B. Chitty. *From the Folks Who Brought You the Weekend: A Short, Illustrated History of Labor in the United States.* New York: New Press, 2001.

Papke, David Ray. *The Pullman Case: The Clash of Labor and Capital in Industrial America.* Lawrence: University Press of Kansas, 1999.

Pelling, Henry. *American Labor.* Chicago: The University of Chicago Press, 1960.

Raddock, Maxwell C. *Portrait of an American Labor Leader: William L. Hutcheson.* New York: American Institute of Social Science, 1955.

Rayback, Joseph G. *A History of American Labor.* New York: Free Press, 1966.

Sinyai, Clayton. *Schools of Democracy: A Political History of the American Labor Movement.* Ithaca, N.Y.: ILR Press, 2006.

Ware, Norman J. *The Labor Movement in the United States, 1860–1895: A Study in Democracy.* New York: Vintage Books, 1955.

Weinstein, Allen. *Freedom and Crisis: An American History.* New York: Random House, 1974.

FURTHER READING

FURTHER READING
Bartoletti, Susan Campbell. *Kids on Strike!* Boston: Houghton Mifflin, 1999.

Flagler, John J. *Labor Movement in the United States*. Minneapolis: Lerner, 1990.

Freedman, Russell. *Kids at Work: Lewis Hine and the Crusade Against Child Labor*. New York: Clarion Books, 1994.

Kurland, Gerald. *Samuel Gompers: Founder of the American Labor Movement*. Charlotteville, N.Y.: SamHar Press, 1972.

Marcovitz, Hal. *Cesar Chavez*. Philadelphia: Chelsea House, 2003.

Stearman, Kaye. *Child Labor*. Chicago: Raintree, 2003.

White, Anne Terry. *Eugene Debs: American Socialist*. Chicago: Chicago Review Press, 1974.

Worth, Richard. *Dolores Huerta*. New York: Chelsea House, 2006.

WEB SITES
ALF-CIO: America's Union Movement
www.aflcio.org

The Dramas of Haymarket
www.chicagohs.org/dramas/overview/overIntro.htm

Child Labor in America 1908–1912,
Photographs of Lewis W. Hine
www.historyplace.com/unitedstates/childlabor/index.html

Samuel Gompers: First President of the American Federation of Labor, 1886–1924
www.kentlaw.edu/ilhs/gompers.htm

Chicago Anarchists on Trial:
Evidence from the Haymarket Affair
www.memory.loc.gov/ammem/award98/ichihtml/hayhome.html

Knights of Labor
www.phoenixmasonry.org/masonicmuseum/fraternalism/knights_of_labor.htm

American Labor: Song about the U.S. Labor Movement
www.songsforteaching.com/mme/americanlabor.htm.

Women and Unions: Late 19th Century Labor Organizing by and for Women
www.womenshistory.about.com/od/worklaborunions/a/late_19th_cent.htm

PICTURE CREDITS

PAGE

INDEX

ABOUT THE AUTHOR

TIM McNEESE is associate professor of history at York College in York, Nebraska, where he is in his sixteenth year of college instruction. Professor McNeese earned an associate of arts degree from York College, a bachelor of arts in history and political science from Harding University, and a master of arts in history from Missouri State University. A prolific author of books for elementary, middle, and high school and college readers, McNeese has published more than 90 books and educational materials over the past 20 years, on everything from Picasso to landmark Supreme Court decisions. His writing has earned him a citation in the library reference work *Contemporary Authors*. In 2006, McNeese appeared on the History Channel program *Risk Takers/History Makers: John Wesley Powell and the Grand Canyon*. He was a faculty member at the 2006 Tony Hillerman Writers Conference in Albuquerque, New Mexico, where he presented on the topic of American Indians of the Southwest. Professor McNeese was a contributor to the 2007 *World Book Encyclopedia*.